Nurturing Reflective Christians to Teach

A Valiant Role for the Nation's Christian Colleges and Universities

**The proceedings from the first National Symposium
for Nurturing Reflective Christian Teachers**

April 7-9, 1994
Trinity Christian College

Edited by
Daniel C. Elliott

With Foreword by
Arthur F. Holmes

University Press of America, Inc.
Lanham • New York • London

Copyright © 1995 by
University Press of America,® Inc.
4720 Boston Way
Lanham, Maryland 20706

3 Henrietta Street
London, WC2E 8LU England

Library of Congress Cataloging-in-Publication Data

National Symposium for Nurturing Reflective Christian Teachers (1st : 1994 : Trinity Christian
College, Palos Heights, Ill.)
Nurturing reflective Christians to teach : a valiant role for the nation's Christian colleges and
universities : the proceedings from the first National Symposium for Nurturing Reflective
Christian Teachers, April 7-9, 1994, Trinity Christian College / edited by Daniel C. Elliott ;
with a forword by Arthur F. Holmes.
p.   cm.
Includes bibliographical references.
1. Church and education--United States--Congresses. 2. Teachers--Training of--United States-
-Congresses. 3. Christian education--United States--Philosophy--Congresses. I. Elliott, Daniel
C. II. Title.
LC379.N38   1995
377'.1--dc20   94-47063 CIP

ISBN 0-8191-9869-2 (cloth: alk.paper)
ISBN 0-8191-9870-6 (pbk: alk paper)

Contributing Presenters:

Doug Blomberg	National Institute for Christian Education, Mt. Evelyn , Australia
John Chesky	Montreat-Anderson College, Montreat, North Carolina
Daniel C. Elliott	Azusa Pacific University, Azusa, California
Patricia Murphy Long	Malone College Canton, Ohio
Ken Pudlas	Trinity Western University Langley, British Columbia
James K. Rooks	Redeemer College, Ancaster, Ontario, Canada
Linda L. Samek and Grant M. Tipton	Western Baptist College, Salem, Oregon
James E. Schwartz	Geneva College Beaver Falls, Pennsylvania
Harro Van Brummelen	Trinity Western University, Langley, British Columbia

Dedication

This work and all of its subsequent applications are dedicated to our Lord and Savior Jesus Christ, who presented us with the command to enable the little children to come to Him. It is further dedicated to all Christians who labor in public and private schools, striving against increasing odds to model Christ with devotion and excellence.

Contents

Foreword

Arthur F. Holmes

In The Abolition of Man, C.S. Lewis discusses a secondary school writing textbook whose authors treated value statements as referring to nothing more than the emotional states of the speaker. Intentionally or not, "under cover of teaching English," Lewis declares, they are propagating their philosophy. Interestingly, he labels this text "The Green Book," echoing the labels students gave to Wittgenstein's "Blue Book" and "Brown Book." His point is that whether or not you think much about world views, they do, in any case, affect what you do. And *world views affect the education of prospective teachers.*

A world view consists of either tacit or conscious beliefs, values and attitudes, a more or less coherent framework of reference. It affects educational objectives, curricular decisions, the selection and handling of course content, teaching methods and student guidance. The moral is plain: be sure prospective teachers learn to identify the worldview assumptions at work in learning theories, textbooks, pedagogies, etc. Give them experience in what James Sire calls "world-view analysis": as in value analysis we look at what underlies behavior patterns, so in world-view analysis we must learn to identify assumptions that undergird the language, the methods, the ideas of a writer, and of course to shape our own practices and work conscientiously in the light of a Christian world view.

For teachers, the key area of a world view is the nature of persons. Plato's elitism focused on the rational, contemplative type who can be educated to practice the rule of reason, and his educational proposals followed accordingly. Rousseau's proto-Romanticist individuals should be free to act "naturally." Dewey saw evolving social organisms adjusting to problem situations, and so set out to educate "problem solvers," while B.F. Skinner's determinism required operant conditioning towards behaviorally defined objectives. Whatever merit there may be in these ideas, they all reflect larger world views that are far from Christian.

What then is so different about a Christian view of persons? Over the years I have listened to faculty candidates address that question, usually as if they have never considered it in this sort of context before. The typical response is the empirically obvious—we are sinners. (G.K. Chesterton says that original sin is the one empirically verifiable Christian doctrine). But is this all? How might we "unpack" the image of God in relation to teaching? I would emphasize that, like God, a person is *basically a relational being*. This is a main theme throughout the Biblical literature, in opposition to the excessive individualism of the West which tends to regard us all as Robinson Crusoes independently fending for ourselves. Daniel Defoe knew what he was doing, he was after all a social philosopher and reflected the views of his day: Thomas Hobbes and John Locke had extended the atomism of mechanistic science to human society, so that all of us have an independent existence, by nature so, and social entities like families and states exist only on a contractual basis. In his **Second Treatise on Civil Government**, Locke made even marriage something we enter into "by reason" rather than "by nature." Descartes had made thinking the private activity of a solitary individual, rather than a dialogical process, and Kant insisted on the autonomy of reason apart from the desires and interests that link us to others, making rational autonomy the final point of appeal in ethics. A person's identity in this tradition is carried by her own conscious memory, a private and individualized thing, rather than being defined by the relationships (family, community, occupation, etc.) that make her what she is. Liberty then becomes the maximization of individual freedom to do whatever one wants, limited only (says J.S. Mill) by what would harm others. We see the outcome in Robert Bellah's **Habits of the Heart**, in the tragic fruit of psychological and ethical egoism.

From a historical point of view alone, this kind of individualism is a tragic aberration. The Greeks and the medievals knew better (remember Aristotle: we are social animals). So do African and Asian cultures. So does Continental European thought since Hegel: think of his master-servant relationship and its necessity for the individual identity of both, or think of Buber for whom "I-thou" is the basic term, not "I" and not "Thou." Carol Gilligan is, then, closer to the truth than

Lawrence Kohlberg, not only on moral development but also on the nature of persons.

From a Biblical point of view, too, my identity is relationally rooted. I exist in relation to God in and through other relationships: to the physical world, to family and work and community, and to the church— on all of which I depend and of which I am, in all my daily being, a part. We are responsible agents in all these relationships, not independent but interdependent. Is not this the Biblical picture of persons?

What educational implications does this kind of world view thinking suggest" We should not be surprised that learning is greater in groups than alone, and should plan class activities accordingly. What kind of understandings are needed? Plainly an understanding of society, its structures and processes and problems, of family especially, of social and physical environments, and of our mutual and individual responsibilities therein. And what kinds of skills? Communication skills, conflict resolution skills, group decision-making skills. And what types of values? Civility? Loyalty? Respect for others? Caring? That is, not so much the skills and values of the autonomous individual, as those of group participation. Chickering's concept of integrity also increases in importance: consistency from day to day, external behavior consistent with inner thoughts and feelings, responsibly engaged in every area of one's life.

Other foci beside the person are essential in a Christian worldview, of course, like the goodness, power, and fragility of creation in its unfolding possibilities we glimpse through the arts and sciences and in our social institutions. In teaching teachers to think Christianly, however, some goals are already clear:

1. Develop an understanding and appreciation of where a Christian world view differs, and where it is akin to, its competition.
2. Develop the ability to identify and evaluate assumptions and values in educational materials, theories, and methods.
3. Develop the ability to operationalize (for curriculum, pedagogy, etc.) educational implications of a Christian world view.
4. Develop a professional identity that models the personal and educational outcomes of a Christian world view, recognizing that teaching is a strategic calling for God's people in this world.

Acknowledgments

The first gathering of a few "nurturers of *reflective Christian practitioners* was facilitated by some wonderful teacher-educators. Trinity Western University's Harro Van Brummelen and Calvin College's Gloria Stronks contacted Teacher-educators from Christian Colleges throughout North America and even in Australia. Through their efforts a "world-class" group of teacher educators gathered to share the fruits of selected investigations into the topic: *What should Christian teacher educator institutions be doing to nurture reflective Christians to serve as classroom teachers?* The group promises to continue the investigation, to meet again in two years, and to expand. The question and answers are complex but vital.

Acknowledgment is also given to the President and staff of Trinity Christian College for hosting the conference, and for providing excellent meals and meeting places for the group. Our gratitude goes especially to Liz Rudenga who looked after many of the logistics of the conference.

Finally, we appreciate the dedicated and enthusiastic teacher-educators, most from member institutions of the Christian College Coalition, who gave their time and traveled from far to make this conference amost enriching time for us all.

Institution and Project Participant
Azusa Pacific University, Azusa, CA: Daniel C. Elliott

Bethel College, St. Paul, MN.: Claire Henry, Terry Lawrence

Bluffton College Bluffton, OH: Richard Hansgen

Calvin College, Grand Rapids, MI: Peter DeBoer, Gloria Stronks

Covenant College, Lookout Mountain, GA: Donovan Graham, Stephen Kaufmann, Rebecca Dobson, Tim Evearitt

Dordt College Sioux Center, IA: Jack Fennema, John Van Dyk

Durham Christian Secondary School, Ontario, Canada: John Hull

Geneva College, Beaver Falls, PA: James Dittmar, Romaine Jesky-Smith, James Schwartz

George Fox College, Newberg, OR: Gary Kilburg, Beth La Force

Huntington College, Huntington, IN: Sharon and Steve Holtrop, Jonathan Parker

Institute for Christian Studies, Toronto, Canada: Ken Badley

John Brown University, Siloam Springs, AR: Sandra Van Thiel

Malone College, Canton, OH: Patricia Long

Montreat-Anderson, Montreat, NC College: John Chesky

National Institute for Christian Education, Mt. Evelyn, Australia: Doug Blomberg

Northwestern College, St. Paul, MN: Ron Juffer

Redeemer College, Ancaster, Onteario, Canada: Jim Rooks

Trinity Christian College, Palos Heights, IL: Liz Rudenga, Steve Vryhof

Trinity Western University, Langley, British Columbia, Canada: Joy McCullough, Ken Pudlas, Harro Van Brummelen

Western Baptist College, Salem,OR: Linda Samek

Westmont College, Santa Barbara, CA: Sally Webb

Wheaton College, Wheaton, IL: Arthur Holmes, Jillian Lederhouse, Richard Turner

Introduction

The 1990's are years of social reorganization and reorientation. It seems that all values and social standards are up for review and re-certification. Ideologies across the spectrum from ultra-conservative to ultra-liberal are pulling apart the fabric of Western society, leading to political conflict and multiple polarization. Schools of education are caught up within this cyclone of sometimes violent controversy. As society debates just what it is that students should learn, and what processes should be used to teach them, teacher-educators find themselves pulled in the direction of their inner *world view*.

In the spring of 1994 teacher-educators from representative institutions within the Christian College Coalition met in Palos Heights IL to consider the issues involved in preparing teacher candidates. The *Christian* world view orientation calls for us to prepare individuals who are inherently *Christian* in their approach to their students and professional colleagues. But defining and explaining the *Christian* world view, as relates to professional education, needs a great deal of careful consideration.

Just what is it that *Christian* colleges of education should do in preparing teachers for the nation's schools? How will our particular approach be uniquely appropriate to the challenges faced by education in this era of conflict and change? Building on the excellent frame of reference laid down for us all by the eminent scholar, Arthur F.

Holmes, the papers presented in this volume begin to answer that question.

Daniel C. Elliott, of Azusa Pacific University, Azusa, CA, reviews the literature and the holy Scriptures to identify essential ideals that could serve as guides when dealing with public education. He asks and answers the question "Should we teach Christian doctrine, or should we teach Christianly?"

Harro Van Brummelen, from Trinity Western University, in British Columbia, argues for the need of a new general curriculum course to counter the increasingly destructive influence of a secular culture in order to help students reflect on and experience how a Biblical world view impacts the way we plan curriculum and choose content, methods, and resources. His chapter demonstrates how teacher-candidates may develop a personal curriculum orientation that guides their curriculum practice.

James Schwartz of, Geneva college, presents an inspiring consideration of mathematics instruction as reflecting the perfection of Creator God. He describes a two-course sequence for preparing elementary teachers in mathematics so that they may reflectively instruct pupils within a distinctively Christian world view of the nature of mathematics.

James K. Rooks, of Redeemer College in Ontario, Canada, explores the development of reading-teacher knowledge and decision-making abilities in pre-service teachers. He considers how we as teacher-educators can enable future teachers fidelity to the vision of teachers-learners as images of God.

Ken Pudlas, also of Trinity Western University, examines the importance of the Christian imperative for unconditional love as it relates to special needs students. Lamenting the failure of individuals within Christian community to openly accept individuals who are *different*, who need special care, or do not fit a neat and tidy expectation of the "good student," Pudlas cites both educational literature, and holy writ which requires us to prepare teacher-candidates who will exercise unconditional love, and give whatever it takes for meeting the needs of learners.

Linda Samek, of Western Baptist College in Salem, Oregon, presents findings from research done by her and Grant Tipton III, concerning use and belief in efficacy of reflective practices by education faculty members. The very interesting question is posed as to just how reflective *we* teacher-educators are in *our* practice of education.

Patricia Long, of Malone College, Canton, Ohio, reviews Christ's teachings for models and examples that our teacher-candidates might use to encourage higher order thinking and inquiry learning strategies with their pupils.

Doug Blomberg, of the National Institute for Christian Education, in Australia, presents us with a "down under" analysis for preparing teachers who can reflect a Biblical view of knowing and learning. Blomberg examines the artistry of teaching, as it requires our teacher-candidates to be articulate. He further considers the craft of teaching, requiring technical expertise. All this he relates to the essence of the Christian world view as it uniquely directs our preparation of teacher-candidates.

John Chesky, of Montreat-Anderson College, in Montreat, North Carolina, steeping his thinking in communication theory, explains a three-tiered foundation for developing reflective Christian practice. Rhetorical specification equips teachers with "handles" for deciding upon what they must reflect (self, content, methods, audience, purpose, and context). Decoding theory helps teachers understand why reflectivity is necessary. Finally, Christ's love teaches how to reflect and therefore how to decode more accurately.

This volume is not the answer, but merely the beginning of a framing of the questions to be asked. The group that met, has committed to organize and repeat the process every two years, in order to establish an ongoing forum for Christian teacher-educators to examine and formulate an educational-preparation theory that is distinctly *Christian*. The succeeding gathering of scholars to continue investigation is anticipated for the Spring of 1996. A call for papers will be presented to all member institutions of the Christian College Coalition, and previous participants.

Daniel C. Elliott, Ed.D., Editor

Chapter 1

To Teach Christianity or To Teach Christianly, That is the Question!

What should the priority be for Christian colleges of education in preparing candidates for the public schools?

Daniel C. Elliott
School of Education
Azusa Pacific University, Azusa, California

Introduction

Public Schools, the Focus of the Argument

Teachers in America's public schools have an awesome responsibility--that of shaping our society. That fact is well known by members of every philosophical orientation which makes up our diverse cultural mosaic. Many in our society, regardless of their personal "religious views" are beginning to recognize that we have lost basic values, and that we lost them at the instructional levels in both family and schools (Coles & Genevie, March 1990). Throughout the last several decades we Christians have whined and complained about this loss, while doing little to correct the problem except, perhaps, to separate and segregate ourselves deeper within our Christian enclaves and private schools (Sidney, 1989).

Christian evangelicals and moderates are awakening to the need for actively reinfusing Christian values and heritage into *public* education. In the public arena, however, these efforts can be spearheaded by non-educators, non curricularists, and people who do not fully perceive the overwhelming mission laid at the door of public schooling. The objection, it seems, has been that some have wanted to make *religious* information, doctrine, and dogma a *part of the curriculum*, and essentially "religious" activities a part of the classroom activity.

Many Christians decry the inappropriate application of the so-called doctrine of "separation of church and state." Christians, of late, have been voicing their frustration at the political/educational system that has in fact instituted a *religion of secularism* in the school content, by the deliberate exclusion of: religious views; accurate historical treatment of religious heritage in our history; and the pressure to muzzle those teachers and administrators who personally hold *Christian* views. And yet, there has been a clear over reaction to the problem(Barton, 1991). *Separatists* continue to call upon Christians to abandon the public education system, and replace it with a completely isolated, religious and sectarian training.

In his somewhat one-sided treatise, <u>God's Choice </u>(1986) Alan Peshkin, a Jewish, non-Christian, examined the isolated world of the private Christian church school community. He suggested that there appeared to be a functional *and purposive* difference between the Christian School and the Public School. For Peshkin, the sectarian Christian school was totally and wholly devoted to the development of character, with academic learning only a characteristic of character. He described the public school as an institution devoted to what he called "humanism", mistakenly associating with what his Christian subjects fear as *secular humanism*. Unfortunately, Peshkin totally misunderstood the nature of humanism as an approach to learning, errantly choosing to juxtapose it with Christianity.

What Peshkin failed to recognize was that in the public schools Christians abound! The same world views that the Christians would have in our private Christian schools can certainly be found among Christian teachers in public schools. Christian's are Christians, if they are Christians at all. He misapplies the notion of "humanism" in his description, as do most of those within the church of Christ who make a practice of attacking the public school.

Understanding Multiple-Model Lesson Design

Teaching has never been a greater challenge. Our society seems to be falling apart at the seams. The conflicting pressures and expectations by the diverse members of our public place schoolers in a pressure cooker of controversy. Today's teacher needs to have a quiver full of strategies and methods to apply the the many special needs of their clients. Teaching has gone through a period of reorientation over the last several decades. The move away from subject based content into student-centered and problem based content has taken us through a reform of instructional methodology. In the 1970's and 80's huge efforts were made to define the practice of teaching in steps, as illustrated most often by the work of Hunter, Russell, and Rosenshine. (Hunter, 1976, Ehrgott & Luehe, 1984) A process of improvement on the traditional lecture approach to teaching came to be seen as "direct instruction."

But additional investigation revealed quite a number of other very successful approaches to teaching, including but not limited to: concept attainment, concept development, advance organizer, cooperative inquiry, cooperative learning, jurisprudential investigation, Socratic inquiry, or process writing (Joyce & Weil, 1986, Gunter, et. al. 1990, California, 1990).

The exciting discovery of this new methodological diversity was that creative teachers need not be bound by a *bureaucratically prescribed* method for delivering their lessons. Teachers could be free to draw upon the science of teaching, simultaneously expressing instructional artistry as they *designed* lessons aimed at improving specific students with specific needs. Teachers can create a *blended model method* of teaching, drawing from the several models in their quiver, crafting a specific method to hit a specific target. The metaphor of the quiver suggests the similarity between teachers and expert archers who craft specific types of arrows for specific conditions and targets. Teachers are the expert archers who send specially crafted pedagogical missiles along a precisely determined trajectory to meet a specific need. (Elliott, 1994)

Looking to Jesus' instructional activities as models for teaching, we notice that he carefully crafted his approach to his learners according to the diagnosed need. He did not treat every learner or group of learners, with a uniform general approach. On the hillside he proclaimed truths for enhanced living, and for living as citizens of the new spiritual kingdom. With the woman at the well he used Socratic inquiry to draw her attention to her past, and thus to her need. With the people he used parables and metaphors that they could understand and relate to. With his disciples he posed problem-based circumstances asking them to solve them and then commented upon their solution. He never once began his lesson with a *statement of objective* (i.e. "today, in this lesson we will consider the seven necessary viewpoints of the Christ's messengers" as a prelude to his teaching in Matthew, Chapter 10, when he instructed the Disciples and sent them out in pairs).

One gets the feeling that Jesus would have a hard time achieving tenure in our schools today, because he did not consistently employ a seven-step lesson plan with behaviorally described instructional objectives in the cognitive domain. He would, it seems, need a strong remediation plan monitored closely by the principal.

What do you mean *Christian Humanism?*

There is a branch of educational psychology termed *humanism* which suggests that we treat learners as individuals, separate and complex human beings with hierarchical needs that direct their behavior. It calls for teachers to be sensitive to the students' world, self-concept, self-esteem and holistic developmental stages. Learning must be delivered through warm, friendly, and democratic student-teacher interactions, minimizing coercive and strict disciplinary measures (Ornstein & Hunkins, 1993). Students work through group inquiry, and in a problem based curricular design involving diverse subjects like language arts, science, and math.

Humanists call for curriculum and teaching to be accomplished in an integrated process, taking life as its model. Christ's model for teaching was *always* this. Never did the Lord lecture on history, or drill his learners on math facts. Nowhere did he call upon learners to recite memorized facts, states, and capitals. His entire curriculum and instructional deliver was centered around the real needs that real human beings have for daily relationships, and for the most important eternal relationship— with our Heavenly Father.

Secular Humanism

There is a quasi religious doctrine called "Secular Humanism" with which many evangelical Christians errantly identify *all public schools* and public school teachers.. Secular humanism is the belief that there is no supreme being, and that *collective mankind* focused with positive energies and for positive motives is the *force* we have formerly thought of as *God*. (Elliott, 1991) This view suggests that there is within all persons the capacity to overcome adversity if we can simply reach deep enough inside our psyches.

Secular humanism tells us we need no god for we become the captains of our ships of life, and the masters of our own destinies. None of this is even remotely connected to the principles of humanistic psychology or views of learning. The only possible connection might be that some who are psychological humanists view human nature as inherently good, not recognizing the *fallen* nature of man as seen by others of more conservative philosophies and as particularly foundational to the Judeo-Christian world view.

Humaneness, Humanism, and Christ-likeness

If we view the untapped potential inside us as a gift from God, as part and parcel of the *image of God*, then we can more accurately define each person as a separate and distinct individual, complex and wonderfully made. The psalmist told us *"I praise you because I am fearfully and wonderfully made; your works are wonderful, I know that full well* (Psalms 139:14) In this perspective "classroom humanism is not only compatible with the Christian perspective, it *is* Christian perspective" (Garlett, 1985, p 55).

Christians often go to great lengths to debate and defend the dual nature, divinity and humanity, of the Lord. Yet we seem afraid to use the term humanity to define ourselves and our aspirations, as though we seek to become *inhuman.* Not that we treat people like all other people treat people, for that is to seek to be distinctly "human" in all of it's ugliness. Humanistic psychology suggests rather "humaneness" rather than humanness. Jesus suggested it best in Matthew 7:12, that we *"do to others what you would have them do to you."* In other words, teach your students and interact with them like you want to be taught and interacted with. And permit your students to interact with their teacher as you want to be permitted to interact with your teachers.

George Van Alstine (1982)—a pastor who has for years served his community as a school board member and president—is a fervent evangelical Christian. In his (now out of print) book, Christians in the Public School, Van Alstine described the teaching-Christian in terms of "pre-evangelism, preparing souls for a later work by another servant of the Lord." He explained a recommended process for "Golden Rule sharing of faith and moral value in a public school, suggesting that the Christian who teaches should address such matters in the same way that he or she would want the Buddhist, Islamic, or Atheist who teaches next door to share with the Christian teacher's own children." For Van Alstine, the Christian in the classroom is a lot like leaven in a lump of dough (Luke 13:21). The leaven is hidden in the dough. It is barely perceptible, yet it has a very strong influence on the outcome of the bread-making process.

Van Alstine suggested that Christians have a much greater potential for *spreading* the gospel by following Christ's example, than by trying to turn public school rooms into Sunday-school or Sabbath-school sessions. The most powerful witness a Christian can bring is to confront a learner with the person of Jesus. Show me Jesus, don't just tell me about him. Let me see him through your actions. The role of Christian colleges of education is to prepare future teachers who are able to do just that.

Some conservative evangelical Christians who cannot afford private schools, or who feel a sense of commitment to general public schooling, are calling the faithful to prayer for schools (Nichols, 1990) and for political pressure to identify and reinfuse into the curriculum Biblically-based values, inherent in the Judeo-Christian world view (Garlett, 1985; Dobson & Bauer, 1990; Elliott, 1992). The rhetoric is heating up and the lines are being drawn all across the nation.

Our public schools are not *Christian* schools. They were not intended to be Christian schools. While there was much more general acceptance of what we might term Christian world view, in the beginnings of American public education history, and while the Bible was more openly used in the curriculum, still the sole intent was to produce an educated citizenry. Our intent—we who teach in public classrooms or who prepare those who teach in public schools— should not be to "Christianize" our public schools. Instead, it should be our intent *to be Christlike*. The qualities of effective schools are uniquely aligned with the characteristics of Jesus Christ. When we make Christ our personal "principal" then these characteristics are within the reach of those schools in which we serve.. We need teachers who are Christians, and who model quiet Christianity, rather than noisy Christianity.(Garlett, 1985)

As an evangelical, conservative Christian, and a career public educator, it seems to me that this would be an appropriate time to pause in the debate and re-examine just what the *Bible* actually says that could serve us as fair and appropriate guidelines when dealing with general public education. As I look at the life and teachings of Jesus Christ, and of those teaching disciples that He trained, I think I see more of an emphasis on the "how" of teaching, rather than the "what." If we are Christians who believe that God has placed us in the public school to minister, shouldn't our teaching processes, our discipline processes, our lifestyle reflect who and what we claim to be?

Biblical Guides for Public Schoolers

A teacher's job sometimes seems *impossible*. The apostle James told us *"Not many of you should presume to be teachers, my brothers, because you know that we who teach will be judged more strictly"* (James 3:1). Christians who teach must be prepared to meet the challenges of teaching in today's classrooms. It is essential that they be beyond reproach. *"Live such good lives among the pagans that, though they accuse you of doing wrong, they may see your good deeds and glorify God"*... 1 Peter 2:12) They must exhibit the best that pedagogical preparation has to offer. They must put *more* into their preparation as teachers than the best of the non-Christian world who also have a vision for teaching our offspring. *"And whatever you do, whether in word or deed, do it all in the name of the Lord Jesus, giving thanks to God the Father through him."* (Colossians 3:17)

The Christian is in a very unique position, with a perspective on people that can only come from God. In Colossians 3:12-17 we read: *"Therefore, as God's chosen people, holy and*

> *dearly loved, clothe yourselves with compassion, kindness, humility, gentleness, and patience. Bear with each other and forgive whatever grievances you may have against one another. forgive as the Lord forgave you. And over all these virtues put on love, which binds them all together in perfect unity.*
>
> *Let the peace of Christ rule in your hearts, since as members of one body you were called to peace. And be thankful. Let the word of Christ dwell in you richly as you teach and admonish one another with all wisdom... And whatever you do, whether in word or deed, do it all in the name of the Lord Jesus, giving thanks to God the Father through him."*

This passage of holy writ gives us seven excellent guides for the conduct of our teachers who would call themselves "Christians: compassion, kindness, gentleness, patience, limitless forgiveness, unconditional love, and peace." Our teachers must have *compassion* for the youngster that others don't want. We shouldn't hear complaints like "Why should I have to deal with those *(fill in the blank)* children? The presence of reflective Christians can help a teaching staff to minimize or eliminate wholesale rejection of "kids like those..." Our teachers must exhibit *kindness* in response to the rude haughtiness or ignorant hostility of today's pubescent youth. There must be *gentleness* in dealing with our youngsters. The teacher should have patience with the crack babies and brutalized children of this generation *bearing with* the children who persistently resist them. There must be *limitless forgiveness* toward what seem to be insults and offensiveness from our confused learners. Our teachers must *love*—uniting themselves with the person of Jesus Christ. The *peace of Christ* must rule in the hearts of our teachers— leaving no room for hostility, pride, or revenge. All this the teacher must do in the name of our Lord: expertly plan the lessons; wipe the snotty noses; listen to the angry, frustrated parents; endure and love the obnoxious teenager; obey and serve with distinction, even under the *ineffective* administrator. The Teacher who would be *Christian* should see his or her position as a calling from God, trusting that God has planted them in their assignment.

Marti Garlett, in her wonderful book, Who Shall Be My Teacher (1985), described a person-centered view of instruction as being sorely needed in schools of the coming century. It follows, then, that Christians are sorely needed in our public schools. *"I have more insight than all my teachers, for I meditate on your statutes"* said the psalmist (Psalms 119:99) Notice that the psalmist did not say "I *teach about* your statutes", but rather he said "I *meditate* on your statutes." The Biblical standard appears to be that the effective teacher must internalize the transforming truths of God's Word, integrating and applying them within himself or herself. As we in the schools of education prepare the person to teach, we deliver human wisdom, knowledge, and instructional process skills, we are like any other school of education in this society. We, however claim to be different.

The university at which I serve, Azusa Pacific University, in Los Angeles, California, has the following mission statement.

> "Azusa Pacific University is an evangelical Christian community of disciples and scholars who seek to advance the work of God in the world through academic excellence in liberal arts and professional programs of higher education which encourage students to develop a Christian perspective of truth and life.

It is important that we prepare Christian teachers who will bring to their classrooms a perspective based upon a Christlike lifestyle and attitude. There is really no place for *preaching* in a classroom, because preaching has little to do with actual learning. The prime strategy to enhance student learning is to merge what is said with what the teacher does—modeling. All experts on teaching agree that modeling is a *sine qua non* of instruction. Whether one teaches children or adults, without demonstration, and an opportunity to practice with low-risk feedback, learning won't happen much (McLaughlin & Marsh, 1978; Joyce & Showers, 1980; Stallings, 1980).

If we say we are given to witnessing for our Christian way of life, then we must do so effectively and efficiently. Preaching is *not* the proven way to do so. *"...I will show you my faith by what I do"* (James 2:18*b*).

UnChristian Case Studies of Christian Teachers

Consider two classroom teachers, observed by Marti Garlett in the mid 1980's. who viewed themselves as "Christian." Our first was a new teacher in a small, mid-American, religious town school. He elected to make his classroom a pulpit. He found every opportunity to infuse his content with religious dogma. He preached and prodded his youngsters to learn about Christ. To him everything in his classroom responsibility became subordinate to *witnessing*. He identified those who were and were not Christians. He assessed the levels success for those whom he had identified as Christians, and advised them strongly on how to live their Christian lives. He began to advise them on their clothing, their make-up, their supposed moral challenges. It was his desire to *scare* them into change by references to God's vengeance, if they failed to follow his admonitions.

Eventually this teacher was fired because he had lost sight of the importance of modeling Christlike love and acceptance. He had become so distracted that he ceased teaching the knowledge, skills, and abilities inherent to the adopted curriculum.

The Bible does not describe our Lord as requiring people to meet special qualifications prior to treating their needs. Rather, he was criticized for associating with the very people who failed to "live up to" the standards of the establishment. Christ accepted people just as they were, and dealt with their needs, as they came up. This teacher had set about to change students spiritual lives before he was ready to address their academic needs.

Our second "Christian" teacher, lets call her "Faith Ruler," made it a habit, at the beginning of each school term, to announce to her students that she was a Christian, telling them that it was important for them to know her stands on certain life's big issues. Though she never again mentioned her Christianity, she took actions repeatedly to define her Christianity— which, in this case, were most unfortunate for those watching and learning from her example.

Faith required everyone in the class to work on the same page at the same time, without any notice of individual ability or need. She persisted in whole class instruction, never once attending to individual differences. She ran the classroom with an almost cruel dictatorialism, permitting not even the slightest individualism on the part of any student. She insisted on an unnaturally silent environment. Any student forgetting the rule of silence ended up with hundreds of punishment sentences, "I will not talk again," as homework. Students in Faith Ruler's class tended to hate the act of writing. Worse, many lost the desire to express themselves on paper, one of the most important and expressive and healing of human communication skills.

Mrs Ruler regularly scolded kids with severe tongue-lashings and public humiliation. She resented and criticized all school support services like reading teachers and special education facilitators, often refusing to permit her students the opportunity to attend sessions which had been arranged for them. Her students, even those from Christian homes, began to recoil from this "Christianity" that they had come to identify with "Mrs. Faith Ruler." (Garlett, 1985)

We must conclude that neither of our two "Christian" teachers were very reflective in their Christ likeness. Teachers must model their belief in the innate importance of *every* child. *"Let the little children come to me, and do not hinder them, for the kingdom of God belongs to such as these"* (Mark 10:14)

Jesus modeled his meaning at this point by taking the children who had formerly been shunned by the adults and holding them in his arms—personal commitment at an almost intimate level. Notice, the master teacher took the child individually in his arms. You can't hold a whole class in your lap, you must do it one child at a time. Teachers must know how to do this. If there is a conflict between what we say, and what we do, then what we do will be the lesson that our students will most notice, and believe.

Garlett (1985) suggested what she called "unnoisy Christianity" as a means practicing what one believes. The teacher who models Christ's love and acceptance; who demonstrates a sensitivity to individual needs and concerns as did our Master Teacher; who treats an audience of learners without losing sight of the individuals in the crowd; this teacher is following in the model of the Master Teacher. *"Whoever welcomes one of these little children in my name welcomes me; and whoever welcomes me does not welcome me but the one who sent me."*(Mark 9:37)

Jesus Christ as The Model Teacher

The characteristics of teaching that we in Christian colleges of education should infuse in our preparation programs can be represented with a strong Scripture base. We refer to Jesus Christ as Master Teacher. He demonstrated the following seven characteristics in his teaching activities: *spontaneity, respect for diversity, a sense of humor, benefits of solitude, joy in creativity, respect for complexity,* and a *delight in teaching.*

Jesus modeled spontaneity.

Scripture is full of incidences wherein the Lord spontaneously interrupted one process to deal with another. Reading about his teaching sessions, throughout the Gospels, one gets the impression that he was looking around as he taught, seizing illustrations from the physical or activity environment as illustrations for his life-changing objectives. His frequent use of parable, metaphor, simile, or parallelism relating to real life experience illustrate his sensitivity to the world around him and a mastery of integrated instruction.

Jesus modeled appreciation for diversity.

"I say to you that many will come from the east and the west, and will take their places at the feast with Abraham, Isaac and Jacob in the kingdom of heaven" (Matthew 8:11). Jesus accepted *all* persons, even those whom the *establishment* had rejected as being *unworthy* Scriptures tell us that Jesus treated individuals with equity, and without regard to their views of self-importance, or their lack of self-esteem, giving to each as he or she had need. His disciples represented fishing, farming, business, government, and other industries of the day. Jesus did not follow the social customs which devalued women, but elevated them to positions of equality. He appeared first to a woman follower, and then to the men, after his resurrection.

Richard Slimbach suggested that effective teachers today should follow what he called "principled multiculturalism." "Try to imagine," he said, "a lone man sitting

> on a hillside telling his Jewish disciples that in the 'Kingdom' he was inaugurating he was not destroying the Law or the [writings and precepts of] the prophets— his disciples' cultural and religious background— but completing it. Was this ultimate authority speaking or consummate madness? Might what was locally applied to the Jews be applied to other nations, cultures, and religious as well? Jesus offered his followers a universal attitude capable of gathering up any good, any truth, any reality found anywhere and then of fulfilling it. The unchanging person and the unshakeable kingdom present us with realities universal enough to not be limited by time, tradition, geography, race, gender, class, or religious creed, yet stable and concrete enough to defy trendy relativisms. As such these two absolutes are not the enemy, but the preserves of any fine trait, tendency, or teaching in

any civilization or "world" of difference. All truth is God's truth"
for God is truth.(Slimbach, 1992)

Jesus modeled a sense of humor.

The Lord used humorous illustrations to make a point. Imagine
the picture of trying to put a camel through the eye of a needle, or of
the five wise and the five foolish girls awaiting the wedding, some
without taking precaution to stock their lamps with oil. There is much
humor in the pages of the New Testament, along with the awesome
task that the Master Teacher undertook on everyone's behalf.. The truly
effective teacher avoids the trap of taking himself or herself too
seriously. This teacher can admit mistakes, can laugh at herself, can
poke fun at himself without losing peace. This teacher can see humor
in stress, but never makes the student the *brunt* of the humor.

Jesus modeled the benefits of solitude.

Often, according to Scripture, Jesus found precious opportunity to be
alone, to pray and prepare for the day, or to reflect upon the one just
completed. It seems that Jesus treasured time alone with the Father,
and time to gather his thoughts both before and after major teaching.
After feeding the thousands in the land of the Gadarenes, Jesus sent the
disciples off in a boat while He went walking up in the hills, alone
with God. Today's effective teacher must resist the crush of daily life,
permitting time to filter and sort out the experiences, as well as time to
gather thoughts and prepare for subsequent teaching demands.

Jesus modeled creativity.

With all of his creative illustrations of eternal truth, utilizing
familiar every day symbols: wheat vs chaff; a son; fertile and unfertile
ground; birds; elements; weather; etc., Jesus demonstrated his
appreciation for creativity. Teachers who creatively approach all
instruction as new opportunities to help learners are modeling a
particular joy for creativity. Teachers who celebrate the success of their
learners by posting student work, praising progress, and looking for
ways to elevate student self-esteem, are being joyous over creativity.

Jesus modeled respect for complexity.

All questions were treated seriously by the Master Teacher. He did not
jump to quick, "pat" answers to seemingly simple problems. He often
took time to probe the situation to aide the learner in better

understanding the scope of his or her question. Life is not ever simple. Complexity abounds and it is the effective teacher's task to help learners to accept complexity, and search out truth amidst complex and diverse challenges. Assisting students in a class to learn to see issues from others' perspective is respecting complexity. Learning to test for real truth, rather than blindly accepting *everything* that is said is respecting complexity. Helping learners to learn skills and abilities in order to solve problems rather than to gain knowledge as an end in itself is also exhibiting a deep respect for complexity.

Jesus modeled delight in the act of teaching.

One can just see the teacher heart in the Master Teacher as he walked among the people, looking for circumstances to help the people, and illustrative material with which to make his lessons. The Gospels record his lessons delivered while he was in transit from one place to another. His classroom was wherever the day found him to be, on a road, in a boat, on a hilltop, in the market place, around a table. *"Jesus then left that place and went into the region of Judea and across the Jordan. Again crowds of people came to him, and as was his custom, he taught them"* (Mark 10:1). The effective teacher today is also always teaching. One who goes by the title "Teacher" will assess learner need as it arises, and grasp upon illustrations and explanations that seem apparent to the learner, then deliver the lesson, either with direct instructions, with inquiry, or by silent-but-purposful example.

Eight Characteristics of Christian Reflectiveness

The well prepared teacher who would teach in our schools, and serve the Lord will do so by having within him or her the very nature of Christ. Those who would effectively teach in the manner of Christ will exhibit eight characteristics as they deliver their instruction and invest themselves into the wholeness of each learner: Empathy, respect, genuineness, warmth, concreteness, confrontation, self-disclosure, and potency.
- *Empathy* is the accurate perception of what students are experiencing as they participate in learning.
- *Respect* is a deep honest appreciation and valuing of each student.
- *Genuineness* is the open and honest expression of oneself, being "real" to the students, rather than some sort of teaching machine that someone turns on at the beginning of each day.
- *Warmth* expresses positive affection for students.

- *Concreteness* explores the depths of experiences relating them thoroughly to the life circumstances of each learner.
- *Confrontation* detects discrepancies between what students say and do and reflects such back to them in ways that enable students to make meaningful change.
- *Self-disclosure* exposes the teacher's personal thoughts, ideas, feelings and experiences at critical moments in the teaching process, assisting students in the relating of knowledge, information, and skill to life.
- And last, *potency* prepares students to have command of themselves, rather than being buffeted by the actions of others, helping students to see that they are indeed responsible for their own actions. (Garlett, 1985)

Golden Rule Class Management Strategies

In another classroom case study we see how words and deeds of a teacher can send a mixed message. During a lesson, John was distracted, not listening attentively, or at least, not understanding the teacher's words. At one point he raised a hand and asked about the instruction. The teacher, stopping abruptly in the middle of an explanation, rolled her eyes in disgust at the interruption and sighed "didn't I just finish explaining that? Where were you *this time* Johnny?" Embarrassed, the boy withdrew and retreated into a shell, confused, and lost, with a decreased desire to publicly admit that he had any questions. Worse, other students in the class probably learned from Johnny's humiliation. Whether they understood or not, most of them would refrain from taking the personal risk of asking a question when they became lost, fearing the public humiliation from the teacher. How would the Master Teacher have handled Johnny's question?

Recall the instance of the rich young ruler, recorded in the book of Matthew (19:16-30). While teaching a group, a young man approached the Lord with a question. Jesus paused in doing what his lesson plan called for, and entered into an impromptu Socratic inquiry with his new learner. After engaging the young man in thoughtful inquiry, Jesus responded to his original question, advising him according to his particular need. Notice, The Master Teacher could have just given the accepted answer to the boy's question, but He didn't. He could have expressed chagrin at the supposed ignorance of the boy for asking what ought to have been obvious, but He didn't do that either. Nor did he exhibit hostility or irritation at being interrupted in the middle of a very important public presentation. Instead, the Teacher quickly composed a string of probing questions designed to reveal this learner's particular individual need. Then, leading the young man into a frame of reference, the Teacher responded thoughtfully and pointedly to the question. The message hit home, though this particular learner did not choose, at that time, to follow the guide— he did get the message, however. The reflective Christian who would teach will manage the classroom with patience, respect, forgiveness, and love.

Patience (without limit)

We who are strong ought to bear with the failings of the weak and not to please ourselves.
(Romans 15:1) The school teacher who would be a servant of the Lord Jesus Christ will need to be prepared with a lifeline to heaven through which he can be continuously recharged with energy, wisdom, and especially patience. The youngsters in most of this nations' classrooms come from circumstances that never before existed in the quantity that they do today. Children and youth are reacting like young, recently planted trees in a hurricane. They are pushed and blown by every wind of controversy, leaned upon by those who make a life habit of abusing others, assailed with the flying debris from storms of political or social unrest, and are often uprooted by forces that are far beyond their control. Their teachers—those who would truly make a difference in their lives— must build wind-breaks for them. Their teachers must be strong while they are weak. Their teachers must be consistent, while the kids are being tumbled across the landscape in search of new roots to hold them fast.

Respect

Another positive trait in a good class management plan is that the teacher shows respect for the student's personhood, with the dignity of paying full attention to his or her comments and responses. Sometimes we can permit ourselves to be distracted by our on-going monitoring and adjustment of the learning situation. We must catch ourselves when we are not listening to our learners but thinking about our next response. The child deserves our full attention.

Back to our young man, Johnny, in the classroom— the teacher could have asked him, smilingly, what he thought the point was to be. The teacher could have next asked a series of questions which reconstructed the train of thought she had covered in arriving to that point in the lesson. She next could have patiently checked his learner's understanding by asking him to recite back what he understood the issue to be. She could have reassured the youngster's mind, by thanking him for the question, allowing that there may be others who were also confused. This is the Master Teacher's model for responding to student questions, even for inattentive students, to demonstrate, in every way possible concern and love for the individual learner. Such a response would fit a plan of positive discipline and behavior modification.

The Apostle, Paul, (Romans, chapter 12) offers several suggestions for teachers relating to *respect*. Verse three suggests that we should think of ourselves with *"sober judgement"*. In verse 10 we are instructed to *"Honor one another above yourselves."* Verse 18 tells us to make every effort to *"live at peace with everyone."* Applied to the classroom, teachers will be well advised to demonstrate this respectful attitude toward each and every one of the students. As *Christian* colleges of education we must strive to instill this universal respectful attitude within our candidates.

Forgiveness

Jesus modeled a very important quality which we as effective classroom managers must not forget. This particular characteristic is best described as "forgiveness." Jesus was able to move past situations where his learners had let him down. He never held a grudge. He never looked down on his learners because he disliked their response from previous days. Today, teachers are often quite up front about our *judgements* of certain students, or families of students. Just sit in a teacher lunchroom and listen to the conversation, (really, gossip) about the students. One can hear well meaning teachers castigate their students to the extent that one would think there is no hope for the student, he might as well be packaged up and mailed to the north pole or somewhere equally remote!

Teachers—especially we who are Christians—must model forgiveness. Every day must be a new day for our learners. We must not *write off* any of these precious youngsters that God places in our daily care. There are no throw-aways in our schools. Whenever one might be tempted to hold a grudge, it might be profitable to envision Jesus standing there asking "Just what is it that this child has done to make you so angry with him? Well, why don't you just charge that to my account, as though it was my doing. But, by the way, how much do you want me to forgive you of?" This imagery should snap even the worst of us out of a bent for retribution. Or how about reviewing Matthew chapter 7, verses 1-2. *"Do not judge, or you too will be judged. For in the same way you judge others you will be judged, and with the measure you use, it will be measured to you.*" Perhaps Chapter 6: verse 14 will set a special tone for you. *"If you forgive men when they sin against you, your heavenly Father will also forgive you. But if you do not forgive men their sins, your Father will not forgive your sins.*"

Love

The Christian perspective about love differs from that of our hedonistic society. The Christian believer says, together with the Lord Jesus Christ, "I will love you regardless of your situation, of what you look like, of how you act, or of how you treat me." People today are in a never-ending quest to *earn love* from other people. Yet Christ *gave* his love without condition. He commanded us to do as he did— *"My command is this: Love each other as I have loved you"* (John 15:12). To discipline a child without love is to not discipline at all, but, rather to abuse. Without love—the selfless looking out for the best interests of the other person— one cannot effect a permanent, positive change in the behavior of another, for one will not have credibility. *Love is patient, love is kind. It does not envy, it does not boast, it is not proud. It is not rude, it is not self-seeking, it is not easily angered, it keeps no record of wrongs. Love ... always protects, always trusts, always hopes, always perseveres. Love never fails.* (I Corinthians 13:4-8)

Consider   A   Reflective   Christian   Teacher

Teacher of the Year, Patricia Ann Baltz is an excellent embodiment of what Christians who teach should be like. "Pann" had taught for several years in Southern California classrooms, absolutely in love with her students. She experienced severe illness, strokes, and paralyses. Noon of this deterred her from her love of teaching. Pann has since been recognized by her district as Teacher of the Year, California as the 1993 Teacher of the Year, as Silcon Valley Technology Mentor, as California PTA Outstanding Teacher, as the L.A. County Self-Esteem Task Force Outstanding Teacher, as the Girl Scouts Outstanding Teacher, and by Walt Disney Co., as National Teacher of the Year. Pann is described by her colleagues, administrators, students and parents of students as being warm, sensitive, thorough, motivational, exciting, tireless, and Christlike.

In her classroom Pann takes risks. She faithfully presents moral ethics, and standards we would term "Christian." She exhibits the Master's love for every students. Because she is so effective with difficult students her administration "rewards" her by giving her more than anyone else gets. Pann never complains, but thanks them for the opportunity to reach more hurting youngsters. Pann reaches them with selfless love.

Pann establishes a positive partnership with parents of her students. She knows them all on a first-name basis and considers them friends. They often contact her to let her know of special circumstances that occur in the student's lives. Pann participates in district and state curriculum development councils, faithfully representing Christian principles without engaging philosophical opponents in hostility. She is known as a "tough peacemaker—you can't fight with her!"

Pann loves to share her discoveries about teaching with others, and mentors many new teachers in her district and around California. She continues to study and be informed about the best practices of teaching. Pann gave me her "Ten Commandments for Teaching" at a recent conference in which we shared the rostrum.

1. Open honest communication.
2. Take risks for the kids.
3. Establish positive partnership with the parents.
4. Continue professional learning.
5. Contribute to curriculum development.
6. See that there are no "dead ends" (content without consequence, no application).
7. Share one's knowledge with others.
8. Be well prepared for teaching lessons.
9   Train new teachers.
10. Speak out publicly for education.

Were you to meet this wonderful, exciting teacher, you would stand in line to have your children enrolled in her classroom. And, you would barely notice her wheel chair, her slightly slurred speech, and that her right side is quite weak and not well controlled. You would, instead, see a joyful teacher who is absolutely in love with teaching. She exhibits the kind of teachers that Christians ought to be.

Conclusion

Roman's chapter 12, discusses the importance of Christians being *living sacrifices*. I can think of no better metaphor for the Christian who teaches. At the core of this concept, the Apostle Paul writes *"Be joyful in hope, patient in affliction, faithful in prayer"* (Romans 12:12) This verse aptly sums up the role of the Christians who teach in our nation's classrooms. At our *Christian* colleges and departments of education, it is our unique task to produce teachers who will fulfill the Apostle's admonition with regard to students, parents, colleagues, and supervisors. Couple this with the 13th chapter of First Corinthians, describing the selfless, unconditional love that God can place within teachers to give to students, and we have the core of the *effective teacher.* The teacher who loves, who perseveres through difficulty, never losing hope, and who will pray without ceasing, will also be the teacher who will attend to individual students, provide a safe and caring environment, prepare very well, and deliver instruction in ways that are most meaningful and relevant to the different students gathered in his or her classroom from year to year.

This investigation began by questioning what it was that we should prepare Christians who will teach to do, to teach the content and implications of the Christian faith, or to deliver the more general content of schooling in a Christlike way, modeling the faith that they hold. The scriptures that have been presented have suggested the latter. Recognizing that there are candidates in our Christian schools of education who, themselves, are not initiates of the faith, yet we have a responsibility to prepare teachers as *only* we can. My thesis is that the Christians who would teach, especially in the public school must be able to demonstrate both effectiveness in teaching and Christ-likeness of mind and heart. The modeling of their Christlike love and caring will teach the Gospel much more effectively than would doctrinal or theological preaching.

We should remember that it is not the teacher's task to *institutionalize* Christian beliefs in the public educational system. Jesus deliberately refrained from establishing a political theocratic government, though the people implored him to do so. We are called to be individual Christians, not to create *Christian* bureaucracies, even within our schools.

By modeling our teacher-candidates after the Master Teacher in: spontaneity, respect for diversity, humor, appreciation of solitude, joy in creativity, respect for complexity, and a delight in teaching, our teachers can be, not only examples of the believers, but examples of *effective teachers*, as well. Through careful understanding of learning psychologies, and educational philosophies, and an accurate discernment of the *prejudices* that some in the Christian community are propagating, our teachers can become peacemakers in their local communities, facilitating communication, rather than conflict. By becoming very well informed about the many applicable approaches to lesson design our teachers will be well prepared to deliver outstanding instruction.   By exhibiting the principles of: limitless patience, universal respect, forgiveness, and love our teachers will manage and maintain outstanding learning environments. What is the role of the Christian college of education in all of this? It is to prepare teachers who can truly be *Christlike* in the classroom.

Reference List

Barton, D. (1991) The myth of separation. Aledo, TX; WallBuilder Press.
Beach, Waldo (1991). Ethical education in our public schools: Crisis and opportunity. The Clearing House 64, (5) 313-315.
Boyer, E.L. (Ed)(1989). New fuel for school reform. In: The blackboard fumble Wheaton, IL: Victor Books.
California Board of Education (1991) Moral and civic education and teaching about religion. Sacramento, CA. California Department of Education.
Coles, R. & Genevie, L. (March 1990). The moral life of America's school children. Teacher Magazine, pp. 43-49. Editorial Projects in Education.
Dobson, J.C. & Bauer, G.L. (1990) Children at risk. Dallas, TX; Word Publishing
Ehrgott, R. & Luehe, F.W.(1984) Target teaching. Visailia, CA; Key Publications.
Elliott , D.C.(1994). A quiver full of teaching models, strategies, and methods. Azusa, CA. Learning Light Educational Consulting Service.
Elliott, D.C. (1992). Moral and civic education: Time honored ideas for educational reform. A paper presented at the Ninth National Congress for Excellence in Public Education, July,1993, Colorado Springs, Co. Azusa, CA. Learning Light Educational Consulting Service
Garlett, M. (1985). Who will be my teacher: The Christian way to stronger schools. Waco TX. Word Books
Gunter, M.A., T.H. Estes, J.A. Schwab (1990). Instruction: A models approach. Boston, Allyn and Bacon
Heie, Harold. (December 1992). Values in public education: Dialogue within diversity. Christian Scholars Review. Grand Rapids, MI.

Hunter, M. (1982). Mastery teaching. El Segundo, CA: TIP
    Publications.
Joyce, B.R., Weil, M., & Showers, B. (1991) Models of teaching.
    Boston, Ma. Allyn and Bacon
Kohn, A. (April, 1991). Caring kids, the role of the schools. Phi
    Delta Kappan, 496-506.
Luehe, F.W. & Ehrgott, R. (1986). Supervision of target teaching.
    Visailia, CA, Key Publications
McLaughlin, M.W., & Marsh, D.D. (1978). Staff development and
    school change. Teachers College Record 80(1):69-94.
Nichols, F. (1990) Mom's in touch international: Mothers meeting to
    pray for their children and.schools. Colorado Springs CO.Focus
    on the Family.
O'Neill, W.F. (1990) Educational ideologies: Contemporary
    expressions of educational Pphilosophy. Dubuque, Iowa,
    Kendall/Hunt Publishing.
Oliver, D. & Shaver, J.P. (1971). Cases and controversy: A guide to
    teaching the public Issues series. Middletown, CT.: American
    Education Publishers.
Ornstein, A. & Hunkins, F.Curriculum foundations, principles and
    issues, 2nd ed. Boston, MA: Allyn and Bacon.
Peshkin, A. (1985) God's choice. The total world of a fundamentalist
    Christian school.. Chicago, IL. The University of Chicago Press.
Purpel, D.E. (1991). Moral education: An idea whose time has gone.
    The Clearing House 64 (5), 309-312.
Sidney, K Ed. (1989) Preface to : The blackboard fumble Wheaton, IL:
    Victor Books.
Slimbach, R. (September 3, 1992). Divinity & diversity: Reflections
    on principled multiculturalism. A paper presented for the Faculty
    Fall Retreat. Azusa Pacific University, School of Education and
    Behavioral Studies.
Stallings, J. (1980). Allocated academic learning time revisited or
    Beyond time on task. Educational Researcher 9(11)11-16.
Van Alstine, G. (1982) The Christian and the public school.
    Nashville, Abingdon (out of print)
The Holy Bible, New international version. Grand Rapids MI.
    Zondervan Bible Publishers

Chapter 2

The Role, Content, and Structure of a General Curriculum Course in Educating Prospective Teachers

Harro Van Brummelen
Trinity Western University
Langley, B.C. Canada

Introduction

Students entering teacher education programs, also in Christian colleges, have been molded by their North American cultural context. This influence is pervasive, yet subtle. Therefore I believe that a general course in curriculum theory and practice is needed. Such a course helps students reflect on and experience how a Biblical worldview impacts the way we plan curriculum, and how we choose content, methods and resources. The course intends to bridge the gap between the analysis done in philosophy of education courses (one of Trinity Western University's three initial "screen" courses) and the specific issues and classroom planning emphasized in subject methods or pedagogy courses.

This chapter first presents my argument for the importance of a general curriculum course. Second, I give a brief description of the design of the course I teach at Trinity Western University, explaining each of my objectives. Finally, I describe three of the many case studies my students discuss in this course.

A Rationale for a General Curriculum Course

In a chapter in *Educating Christian Teachers for Responsive Discipleship* (DeBoer 1993) I showed that successful teacher education programs are collaborative partnership efforts where the stakeholders share a common vision. This chapter addresses teacher-educators in Christian Colleges. Such institutions usually have a clear sense of mission. Unlike large institutions, we have faculty members who are committed to that mission and to quality teaching that supports the mission. As a result, our teacher education programs can reflect a clear sense of vision and purpose. We can foster a shared ethos that fosters collegiality and collaborative relations. As such, as Christian college professors we have a unique opportunity to help prospective teachers become personally and socially responsible reflective practitioners or reflective strategists. We also can help them experience and perceive the profound moral purpose of teaching.

But it is particularly with respect to that moral purpose that we face difficulties. In my experience, prospective teachers in our colleges usually endorse moral and value imperatives for their own lives. They know what is right and wrong for themselves, even if, like ourselves, they don't always live up to their own standards. In recent years, however, many student teachers also believe that to ask others to consider and accept the ethical and value guidelines they believe in themselves would show intolerance. Some of our student teachers, indeed, are reluctant to guide their students openly about values. They avoid dealing with values explicitly, especially in public school situations. Schools, they hold, promote critical thinking and must avoid all indoctrination.

With this position, however, they indirectly promote ethical relativism ("whatever values you choose in your own life is up to you yourself"). They implicitly teach that any value is as good as any other. They echo the views of our government's curriculum guidelines that we must respect and tolerate all views and values in a pluralistic society (although they usually retreat rather quickly when I ask them whether that includes unprovoked violence or religious oppression).

These and other students usually also uncritically accept subjective constructivism, that is, the belief that individuals construct their own personal meaning and knowledge. In our jurisdiction, perhaps more so than in most, such constructivism has become the underlying philosophy of curriculum development. Its basis is that learners actively construct knowledge and assign their own meaning to whatever they learn. Pupils are self-directing, autonomous individuals. They themselves are the source of truth and freedom. Curriculum guides therefore stress process rather than content. They promote values clarification based on personal choice rather than analyzing value dilemmas on the basis of universal value standards.

Other students, on the other hand, particularly those with a fundamentalist background, want to transmit their black-and-white views without giving an opportunity for personal consideration, exploration and growth. They too quickly assume that they have all the right answers, and that by communicating them they will be able to impose their acceptance. But they still often view values as something added to the unbiased content they teach.

Somewhat paradoxically, both groups of students usually unthinkingly accept that knowledge itself is neutral. The first group looks at knowledge as a means to an end, a vehicle to enable students to choose their own meaning in life. What knowledge is used for that purpose is not all that important. That is why in British Columbia's current primary curriculum guides the choice of unit topics is left with the teachers. Whether you make the content focus of learning balloons or the circus or dragons or communities of living things is not all that important. The process rather than the content adds meaning and value. The second group assumes that knowledge is an objective, impersonal body of facts, concepts and insights. At most, it leads to some value questions that we discuss now and then. Neither group grasps how our culture, including our educational approaches and content, embeds values. Neither is aware of the faith in rationality, individualism and materialism that drives our culture and much of our curriculum content.

Now our social context affects each of us and each of our student teachers. Therefore we need to help our students examine their own cultural baggage and where they stand on important value questions. They begin this in philosophy of education courses. But such courses do not go far enough to help our students see how their thinking affects actual school programs (I speak from experience; I teach such a course. There is just not enough time in one semester to have the students grasp all the implications).

What students need is a course where they recognize and experience the impossibility of a neutral curriculum. We need to help them see that the choice of content and methods will affect their pupils and their attitudes toward life. For example, content choice shows them what their teachers hold to be important. Teachers who emphasize classification in a unit on trees promote human rational thought as something of high value. On the other hand, teachers who stress how forest ecosystems can be destroyed or preserved will more likely teach their students to value human care of the environment. Whatever we teach will reflect a spectrum of values: ethical and social ones, but also, for instance, economic and aesthetic ones. A general curriculum course can develop not only an awareness of such values but also helps student teachers to plan curricula based on Biblical ones.

Student teachers must, of course, also learn to be fair about value positions that differ from their own. But fairness does not mean neutrality. They must learn not to indoctrinate in the sense of being one-sided in their presentations or discouraging their students from asking probing questions or from disagreeing with them. But their pupils need to hear from them what they believe about the important issues of life, and their reasons for holding such beliefs. Only then will their pupils learn to make and act on value commitments essential for a compassionate, just and principled society. In other words, prospective teachers need a course where they articulate their own orientation to curriculum based on their worldview. In a general curriculum course, they get opportunities to explore how they can apply such an orientation in their curriculum planning.

"Hell is a forever without commitment," Elmer Thiessen quotes Lewis Smedes in his recent book, *Teaching for Commitment* (Thiessen 1993, 277). Thiessen concludes that we need to restore the dignity of teaching for commitment at both the college and school levels. "Healthy commitment should be the goal of all education" (277). Despite our uncertainty and fallibility, "we need to dare to believe. We need to dare to teach for commitment" (277). We need to dare help our student teachers teach for commitment. Philosophy of education can provide the framework. Methods courses in specific subjects can work out the details. But for student teachers there is a gap between the theoretical and practical that they often do not bridge unless given specific help. A course in general approaches to curriculum planning such as the one I discribe here provides that bridge.

In an overview course in curriculum students have opportunities to investigate the Christian foundations of curriculum. They explore how Biblical views of reality, the person, knowledge and values provide an overall framework for curriculum planning. Students ponder and apply the implications of this framework, and explore how it relates to the many curriculum issues that cut across discipline fields. What values are embedded in the explicit, null and hidden curricula? How can the curriculum do justice to the different aspects of reality and the different ways of knowing (or multiple intelligences)? To what extent and in which ways should the curriculum be integrated? How do we take into account the social context of curriculum? How do we analyze and use resources effectively? How do we implement and evaluate the effect-iveness of our curriculum planning? Without a general curriculum course as a base, students tend to look at courses in methodology for specific subject areas as "grab bags" of goodies, failing to develop a coherent framework, despite our best intentions.

The Design Of A General Course In Curriculum Theory And Planning

I purposely do not teach a general curriculum course in the "logical" order in which I state my objectives. For this course I usually have two 75-minute periods per week. One class focuses on more foundational under-pinnings and conceptual development. The second class considers more practical concerns, at times before we have discussed the relevant theory.

For instance, I ask students very early in the course to read some recent government curriculum documents. Then in groups of four based on their areas of interest they have to put together and present a classroom unit, indicating how they would teach it (a) in a public school, and (b) in a Christian school. Thus during the first few weeks in the course we already address objectives 5, 6 and 9 directly and 7 and 8 indirectly (see the objectives below). Here I stretch students' comfort zones because we have not yet looked even at the ingredients of a good classroom unit. They are still somewhat unsure of what I expect (even though I do give them a one-page outline describing the assignment).

There are a number of reasons for this approach. First, students raise more and deeper questions about what is involved in curriculum planning. They begin to ask, "Why choose one topic rather than another?" or "How do you decide what to include and exclude?" As a result, they consider the importance of thematic statements and objectives. Second, the approach leads to good discussions not only about sound curriculum planning but also about where they are trying to lead pupils in their future classrooms. Third, the students begin to recognize the complexity of all the factors in curriculum planning, and appreciate that curriculum planning is not a neat, linear, step-by-step process. Finally, almost without exception, students come up with worthwhile units. They put a great amount of work into the project. They become confident that they themselves have a large number of good ideas, and also learn the value of brainstorming ideas with colleagues.

It is important, I believe, to keep elementary and secondary oriented students together in a course such as this, regardless of their intended grade-level focus. (In fact, I wouldn't mind having some of our newer college faculty members take it, too, if they had the time!). I find that the interaction helps everyone widen their horizons. Secondary-oriented students benefit from the willingness of their elementary counterparts to try new and innovative approaches. Those planning to teach primary grades learn to be more analytical and evaluative about what they teach, not just deciding to do something because it'll be fun for their students.

Below, I present and explain each of my general curriculum course objectives.

1. To analyze how curriculum is based on and affected by groundings such as worldviews; views of the purpose of education and schooling; views of the nature of knowledge, the learner and learning, and the teacher and teaching; and the social context.

This objective is a strand woven throughout the whole course. A constant question I ask is, "How do you justify your curriculum decisions on the basis of your beliefs about education and schooling?" We use our discussion of the groundings of curriculum to ask whether curriculum plans enhance the understandings needed for exercising responsible discipleship, whether the curriculum is relevant for the students, and whether it meets their pedagogical needs.

2. To examine and critique major curriculum development approaches and orientations, and to investigate their effects on programs, resources and classroom practices.

The course begins by considering four major curriculum orientations. There are many ways of categorizing such orientations. None of them work perfectly since educators seldom fit precisely and consistently into a specific category. But my categorization gives students a handle on common approaches and their strengths and weaknesses.

We consider the academic traditionalist, technical, deliberative and constructivist orientations. We examine how the metaphor used for curriculum and the basic question it asks leads to certain knowledge, learning and value emphases. I give a very brief historical overview, and analyse the strengths and weaknesses of some Christian educators who "fit" into one of these categories: Mortimer Adler and his Paideia Proposal; ACE and its technical, behavioristic methods; Dwayne Huebner and his deliberative approach; David Purpel and his constructivist mixture of Christian and New Age beliefs.

We discuss the values that commonly frame these orientations. Academic traditionalism often promotes not only the importance of disciplined intellectual training but also a faith in rationality that has led, for instance, to a skewed view of "tolerance," one that does not depend on veracity or responsibility. The technical orientation values functional utility and efficiency without recognizing the Biblical view of persons as responsive, responsible images of God. Most though not all those in the deliberative orientation affirm that individuals can locate the source of freedom in and by themselves. Finally, radical constructivists go yet one step further. For them, the only "absolute" values are human freedom and autonomy; all knowledge and values are provisional and subject to change.

3. To define and explore the implications of a Christian worldview, Biblical values and a Biblical view of knowledge and truth as a basis for curriculum that nurtures commitment.

I begin this section by contrasting the programs of three protestant Christian schools: a fundamentalist one with a strong world-flight mentality; an independent school that maintains chapel services and upholds Judaeo-Christian values but whose curriculum closely parallels that of academically-oriented public schools; and a school that bases its curriculum on the conviction that Biblical guidelines apply to all of life.

Because our students also take a compulsory interdisciplinary course on Christian worldview thinking, I approach worldview somewhat differently than such standards works as Arthur Holmes' *Contours of a Christian Worldview* and Walsh and Middleton's *The Transforming Vision*. Instead, I ask what four God-given decrees mean for education: the Great (creation) mandate; the Great Commission, the Great Commandment, and the Great Communion. For the Great Commission, for instance, we discuss the nature "making disciples" and what it means to teach students everything that Christ commanded us: humility, mercy, peace-making, justice and righteousness, responsible stewardship, integrity, compassion, faithfulness, avoiding legalism and hypocrisy.

Before we look in detail at Biblical values and the curriculum, we discuss the difference between nurture and indoctrination. We also look at the values embedded in textbooks (often conforming students to a narrow, consumer-oriented, individualistic autonomy: "Everything is possible when I am me."). We then look at how teachers foster Biblical values without imposing them unilaterally on students. But we don't restrict our discussion to spiritual and ethical values alone. We also think about values in the judicial/political, economic, social, communication, logical, aesthetic, emotional, physical and mathematical realms. We look not only at how values are fostered through the explicit but also through the implicit and null curricula. Finally, we also consider the curriculum implications of a Biblical view of knowledge and truth. Here I emphasize the Biblical notions that knowledge must always be of mind and heart, and must lead to personal response and commitment. Finally, we consider criteria for justifying curriculum choices.

4. To consider the implications of Biblical directives and recent research in teaching and learning for organizing knowledge in the curriculum and teaching the various aspects of reality.

Here we look at categorizations of aspects of reality (or what Phenix and Hirst called realms and forms of knowledge respectively). What does this mean for teaching subjects? for a core curriculum? for subject content integration? We also look at the basic direction of teaching and learning in basic subject areas within the framework that has been established. Included here are the fine arts, religious studies and ethics, and subjects with application emphases. The course makes much use of small group work, and here groups of students work on different subjects, working out and presenting the implications of their readings for specific topics in the subject discipline.

5. To consider the external frames for teachers' personal curriculum planning and implementation.

6. To examine and critique recent curriculum initiatives in schools in local jurisdictions.

Many external factors affect curriculum organization and content choice. We discuss the "frames" given by society's overall expectations, department of education guidelines, school board directives, school administration leadership, parental pressures, and so on. Our future teachers must learn to analyze and critique recent state and regional curriculum initiatives to prevent them from jumping on every new bandwagon. In my jurisdiction, for instance, recent "bandwagons" have included cross-age integrated units, action research initiatives with their implicit constructivist agendas, and specific marketplace skills.

7. To consider the Biblical view of the person and its implications for the pedagogical frame of curriculum planning.

I find it necessary to spend some time on pedagogical principles that affect curriculum planning. I review the four-phase model I developed in my *Walking with God in the Classroom* (Van Brummelen 1988), and we discuss how it applies to curriculum planning. We also look at Kieran Egan's insights into layers of understanding (see, for instance, Egan 1992).

8. To define and consider key questions in curriculum planning, and to use these to develop, defend and apply a personal curriculum orientation.

During the course students gradually develop their own curriculum orientation. I ask them to write it as a talk they would give to parents of their students, showing how what they believe affects their day-to-day teaching. They have to deal with their view of aims of education, knowledge and curriculum content, the values they will emphasize, learning strategies and the role of the teacher, and evaluation methods to be used.

9. To understand why and how curriculum planning is a key dimension of the teacher's role as a responsive and responsible reflective practitioner.

10. To learn how to construct and adapt yearly overviews and classroom units that reflect students' personal curriculum orientations.

Here we go through the four stages of classroom curriculum planning: considering external program frames, planning yearly overviews, designing and adapting classroom units, and day-to-day lesson planning. Most of our time and effort are spent on designing classroom units. It is through practical planning that students best come to grips with basic perspectives that should guide curriculum planning. The steps we consider and use: (1) selecting worthwhile unit topics and determining their scope; (2) articulating intents (thematic statements and objectives, relating these closely to the values you want to teach); (3) designing, balancing and sequencing learning activities; (4) planning a time schedule; (5) selecting and using curriculum resources; (6) planning student assessment and evaluation; (7) implementing curriculum plans; (8) reviewing the unit's likely effectiveness.

One thing I emphasize is the need for finding a "unifying thread" so that for the students the unit is more than a collection of interesting activities. This could be (1) a problem posed about the topic, (2) a narrative format in which students would trace a story line, or (3) the use of a basic theme or values to look at different sub-topics, consolidating the conclusions in culminating activities.

For a grade 4 unit on pioneers, for instance, students might have one of the following "unifying threads": (1) the problem of creating a new life when a group of people arrives on uncleared land; (2) the personal narrative of a particular pioneer family or settlement, with the story line contrasting, for instance, personal resolution, family love and community cooperation with physical hardship, disdain for Indian people and economic greed; or (3) a consideration of different aspects of pioneer life such as providing food, family life, providing services, and community life in terms of key values and how the pioneers exemplified a specific worldview.

Examples of Three Case Studies Discussed in the Course

Below are three typical (and real) cases that provide a basis for discussing curriculum issues in the course. The ones shown here are three of the many provided in a textbook for this course (Van Brummelen 1995).

I   Rick Binder together with five other grade 5 and 6 teachers recognize the natural rhythm of the school year, and therefore plan a unit for the last five weeks of the school year that is different and appealing for their students, and yet not too difficult to teach once they design it. They are concerned about some of the racist attitudes that students display, especially toward the large number of Indo-Canadians in their community. The theme of the unit becomes that loving your neighbor as yourself means celebrating cultural differences and building bridges.

The teachers begin the unit with two activities. First, they ask students to complete a survey of their attitudes (e.g., I think Punjabi clothing is beautiful). Then they act out a skit that included all the racial remarks, slurs and jokes that the teachers had heard over the last year or two. The teachers regroup the five grade 5 and 6 classes into five groups that rotate among the five rooms, three days a week from 10:30 to 12:00. The students all study five "strands": the history of Indo-Canadians in their community, the Sikh religion, contemporary issues facing Indo-Canadian families, food and clothing, and language and music. The strands emphasize concrete experiences: Indo-Canadian speakers, visits to a Sikh temple and the local Sikh market, preparing and eating

Sikh food, music performances, and so on. Each student makes a personal scrapbook, and also gives a detailed evaluation of the whole unit. The final culminating activity consists of the teachers acting out the skit again, but now reacting to comments on the basis of what happened during the previous five weeks.

What were the results of the unit? First, the students addressed an issue affecting the whole community. They had very positive experiences with a different culture group. When they completed the attitudinal survey again at the end of the unit, the results were startlingly more positive. The next school year the teachers found that almost all comments about East Indian culture among the students were positive ones. The unit also stimulated parents to talk and think about their own attitudes. Most responded positively and said they had gained some knowledge and understanding. The school plans to teach a similar unit each year, with the focus on different culture groups.

What are some of the primary values nurtured in this unit? How can teachers use the unit to be bearers of hope?

II   Analyze the unit outlined below. From the short description, can you speculate what the unit's theme would have been? Which type of integration does it illustrate? Suggest how you might structure this unit using the other types of integration.

Glenda MacPhee taught a unit on *Garbage*. She began the unit by discussing the diversity of things in creation and how all things have a place in reality. Her students considered various naturally-occurring cycles such as the food cycle as well as cycles resulting from human activity. They then explored how garbage results particularly from human activity. The students visited a garbage dump to experience how much our society throws away, and investigated how much of what is wasted could be recycled. In the classroom, they decided how they themselves could reduce consumption and reuse products. They implemented an appropriate plan of action. Meanwhile, the students read and discussed a book about an empty lot that its owner planned to sell for a gas station development.

The owner discovered, however, that the lot is not just a place where people dump litter, but that its every nook and cranny contained much life. This story led the students to look for garbage and for life on an empty lot close to the school. The students also began composting their school room garbage, opening it up two months later to see what had happened (the students planted and later harvested some cherry tomato seeds that had sprouted). Throughout the unit, the students used their journals to react to issues as they arose.

III   Scientists genetically engineer human genes into goats who produce scarce human proteins with their milk. They engineer tomatoes that will not rot and salmon that grow ten times faster than normal. They also apply such research to genetic cures for diseases. But this technology gives rise to troublesome questions. Is it right for human genes to be inserted into animals? Can virus genes stitched into plants to increase disease resistance lead to the creation of "superviruses"? What would happen if genetically engineered salmon escape and breed with normal ones? Should parents be able to pay to have genetically superior babies? Should animals, or humans, be cloned? How should governments regulate genetic engineering and its products? Nobel prize winner Michael Smith says he does not have enough expertise to make ethical judgments about this research. Other scientists claim, however, that unwillingness to face the implications means that the commercialization of genetic research is already out of control (*Vancouver Sun*, December 4, 1993, pp. B1-B3).

This describes, in brief, a science development with vast consequences. Should you deal with this issue in your science classroom? If so, at what age levels? Can you think of creative approaches that would help students explore the underlying issues? To what extent should school science deal with the consequences of technology rather than just with scientific concepts and theories?

Conclusion

Student reaction to Trinity Western's general curriculum course has been very positive, although all of them admit the course involves much work. They have weekly readings with written reactions to curriculum case studies. They have a major group oral presentation on how a theme could be taught in a public school and a Christian school classroom using recent department of education guidelines. They have in-class small group assignments almost each week which they display on chart paper or hand in. They plan and design a detailed teacher resource unit (and, on the whole, do remarkably well; almost each year several make their way into unit resource banks for practising teachers). They gradually develop and then write their own curriculum orientation. They also have an individualized take-home examination where they apply what they have learned to various school-based situations.

In short, in this course students think about the foundations of curriculum and their implications without as yet being too concerned about specific subject content. All of these students have volunteered in classroom situations, but almost none have had any curriculum and instruction courses in particular subject areas or any formal student teaching practica. The general reaction to the course is that it is one of the most valuable ones they take prior to their student teaching.

.

References

DeBoer, P., H. Van Brummelen, D. Blomberg, R. Koole and G. Stronks. 1993. Educating Christian teachers for responsive discipleship. Lanham: University Press of America and Toronto: Institute for Christian Studies.

Egan, K. 1992. Imagination in teaching and learning: The middle school years. Chicago: The University of Chicago Press.

Thiessen, E. 1993. Teaching for commitment: Liberal education, indoctrination, and Christian nurture. Montreal: McGill-Queen's University Press.

Van Brummelen, H. 1988. Walking with God in the classroom. Burlington: Welch. Republished by Alta Vista in Seattle [1992].

Van Brummelen, H. 1995. Steppingstones to curriculum: A Biblical path. Seattle: Alta Vista.

Chapter 3

Learning to Teach Elementary Mathematics at Geneva College

James E. Schwartz
Geneva College,
Beaver Falls, Pennsylvania

Background

NCTM Standards

The four integrative standards from the NCTM *Curriculum and Evaluation Standards for School Mathematics* (National Council of Teachers of Mathematics, 1989) mathematics as reasoning, mathematics as problem solving, mathematics as communication, and mathematics as connections form the basis for my vision of how mathematics should be taught. When the NCTM Standards were first published I was an elementary school teacher who was already teaching in ways that were consistent with the Standards. One of the things that I was sure about was that teaching in this way brought me daily *mathematical* challenges as I sought to make sense of the methods children developed to solve problems. I had to think creatively, flexibly, and with great mathematical insight in order to understand children's various methods of solving problems.

One of my earliest thoughts in reaction to the Standards was that it would be extremely challenging, mathematically, for teachers to teach in this way. From this reaction I developed an interest in teacher knowledge about mathematics. A thorough review of the literature revealed that elementary teachers tended to have profound weaknesses in the area of elementary mathematics. It seemed to me that if this were the case there would be serious difficulties in implementing the NCTM Standards.

Research on Teacher Knowledge and Beliefs

For my doctoral dissertation(Schwartz, 1992) I undertook a study of the role of elementary teachers' knowledge of mathematics as it relates to teaching in ways that are consistent with the Standards. I studied teachers' beliefs about the teaching of math, teachers' understanding of math, and the relationship between both of these variables and the teachers' self-reported teaching practice. I found that there was a relationship between beliefs and practice. Teachers who held cognitive beliefs about the teaching of math were more likely to teach in ways that are consistent with the Standards. I found that there was no direct relationship between mathematics understanding and teachers' willingness to teach according to the Standards. Most importantly, I found that there was a small interaction effect. Pedagogical beliefs mediated the relationship between mathematics understanding and teaching. For people with cognitively-guided beliefs, high mathematics understanding was associated with Standards-consistent teaching. For people without cognitively-guided beliefs (behaviorist beliefs) about teaching, high mathematics understanding was associated with a lack of Standards-consistent teaching.

To me this underscored the importance of two considerations in teacher education: (1) beliefs about mathematics and mathematics pedagogy must be addressed, and (2) when our students learn mathematics it must be in the kind of environment we want them to create when they become teachers. Geneva's EDU 330 and EDU 331 were designed with these considerations in mind.

Our goals in creating EDU 330

Our first design goal for EDU 330 was that our students needed a course in the mathematics content of the elementary school. Our second design goal was that this content needed to be presented in a distinctly Christian context. Our third goal was that the teaching should model the methods of teaching that the students will be expected to master in the later methods course. Our final design goal was that the experience would address the affective dimension: students entering the course with negative attitudes and beliefs about mathematics should be helped to overcome them.

Mathematics for Elementary Teachers

The History And Philosophy Component

Constructivism

One of the things that is becoming clear is that a teachers' conception of knowledge will affect how he or she teaches that content. The philosophical presuppositions that a teacher holds will affect teaching, even in ways that the teacher may not be aware of (Ediger, 1992; Ernest, 1989)

The literature of mathematics education has, in recent years, developed a heavily constructivist perspective. According to Narode, "Philosophically, constructivism advocates an epistemology which views knowledge as belief, and truth as anything but absolute." (Narode, 1987 p. 1). Mathematics, in this worldview, is not seen as truth, but as a social construction of humans that has credibility because it works. Mathematics arises out of explanation, justification, elaboration, and persuasion. Each person constructs his or her understanding of mathematics "...through active communication between people with equal authority in their claims to truth." (Narode, 1987 p. 2).

This view of knowledge is at odds with a Christian worldview that declares that God is absolute, and that He is omniscient. If all the treasures of wisdom and knowledge are found in Christ, then Christians find flaws with radical constructivism.

In spite of the Christian's disagreement with a radical constructivist view of the world, a constructivist view of *learning* may be of great help when it comes to teaching mathematics. In terms of ultimacies, constructivism is a flawed philosophy; but in terms of an individual's attempts to learn, a constructivist view may provide some helpful leverage. Therefore, I hold the constructivist view of mathematics learning to be desirable, for pedagogical purposes.

History and Philosophy of Mathematics

Studies of the history and philosophy of mathematics reveal that humans have searched in vain for certainty in mathematics over the centuries. Even in the technologically advanced societies of today, the foundations of mathematics remain a mystery to humans who reject God. Those who insist that mathematics is purely a construction of the human mind cannot explain why such a construction should work as well as it does to predict and explain the functions of the physical world. Those who insist that mathematics exists apart from humans are hard pressed to say *where* it exists without some reference to God.

This state of affairs leaves the Christian in an enviable position. If mathematics *is* a construction of the human mind, then it is to the glory of God that we as His image-bearers would be capable of generating formulae and relationships that reveal and explain the order that *He* has designed into the world. On the other hand, if mathematics exists apart from humans, then it is no problem at all to conclude that it has its existence in the mind of God. Whichever perspective one adopts, and it may be that both have elements of truth, God is glorified. While we do not dwell on such matters in depth in EDU 330, these ideas are examined. The reason for examining these issues is to sensitize the students to the idea that God is not irrelevant in the area of mathematics.

Learning Math In A Standards-Consistent Environment

There are three components to EDU 330. The first component is the historical/philosophical component. The first several class periods are devoted to this component. The second component of the course is the problem-solving/investigations component. Each class period, after the initial several classes, is devoted to one or two mathematical investigations using some kind of manipulative device. (The students purchase the kit, "Start with Manipulatives" instead of purchasing a course text.) During these investigations a community of inquiry is developed. The students are urged to talk and reason together as they solve problems. They are urged to find a variety of methods of solving the problems, and they are expected to be able to explain their thinking to others. There are many requests to justify thinking, and students are urged to challenge one another to justify thinking when necessary. The third component of the course is the production of journals. Each student is assigned to serve on one of five Editorial Boards whose task is to produce a journal of writings on some aspect of the learning of mathematics. Meanwhile, each student is expected to submit original articles to each of the Editorial Boards (other than his or her own board) in the hopes that those articles will be accepted for "publication."

Math as problem solving, reasoning, connections, and communication

It is my contention that we can teach nearly any topic in elementary mathematics by *beginning* our lesson sequence with a problem. Instead of teaching "skills" and then following our instruction with problems to apply those skills, we should begin our lessons with the problems and use those to develop the skills. In this model of teaching, drill and practice have a place, but not until after a concept has been learned with understanding and in the context of problem solving.

A major component of this problem-focused approach to teaching is that many people will come up with many different ways of solving any given problem. Therefore, students are presented with a problem and they are expected to work on it in small groups. Within the groups any method of solving that works is acceptable, as long as everyone in the group understands it and can explain it. As groups solve a problem, they are encouraged to find more than one way to solve it or to show that they are correct. Following group solution times, representatives from several of the groups are asked to share with the rest of the class one of the methods that they used to solve the problem. Any member of the class who does not understand any portion of the method being explained may request further clarification. Occasionally a faulty solution procedure will be described, and again, any class member may challenge the thinking of the group making a presentation. Our goal here is the development of a community of inquiry in which mathematical knowledge is constructed as a social activity.

The Affective Dimension

Why Is It Important?

Most of the students who decide on elementary education as a major do so in spite of rather than because of mathematics. Most of them are far more excited about children's literature than they are about elementary mathematics. With many of them, there are very negative experiences associated with their own learning of mathematics. Fear of mathematics, along with a genuine distaste for the subject, characterize the attitudes of many students. If these attitudes are left unchecked, they will be passed along to another generation of students. The cycle of fear and distaste of mathematics must be broken, and the years in undergraduate preparation would seem to be the logical time to do so.

How Is It Addressed?

Nearly everything about the design of EDU 330 was intended to provide students with a fresh start in mathematical thinking and learning. Many of the mathematical investigations have aesthetic components. Students are taught and urged to talk through their thinking together. Frustrations are shared in common, as are the joys of discovery. The potential for surprise exists in many of the investigations: students are frequently surprised to find out why a mathematical procedure that they learned by rote works. Grading is very generous. Many writing assignments focus on students exploring their emotions and feelings as they solve specific mathematical problems. There is a noticeable absence of mathematical formulae and procedures to memorize.

What Results Have We Had?

The final writing assignment of the term requires students to reflect on their experiences during the course and on the changes that they see in themselves as a result of those experiences. The thoughts that the students express in these essays reveal some profound results. The following quote provides insight into one student's growth in confidence.

Mary: "I remember talking about ratios in class and using the Cuisenaire Rods. I had no recollection of ever learning anything about ratios in my elementary or high school grades. When you talked about ratios and being able to come up with the answer with the Cuisenaire Rods I thought there would be no way I could do it. When I tried that I ended coming up with the right answer and it was so much easier than trying to remember some formula and converting this formula into the numbers that are given and coming up with the answer."

The importance of the affective dimension of the teaching career is highlighted, again by a quote from Mary:

Mary: "Before taking this class I also began to question myself if I was really meant to be a teacher, because I am so bad in math how will I be able to teach it to actual children. After taking this class I have a greater understanding of how math is changing and I know I will struggle with certain concepts, but I have a more positive attitude and believe math being taught this way will excite children to want to learn math."

(Mary wrote 5 and a half pages in "reflections" on the course!)

Carrie revealed that her attitudes changed. One can sense that she is somewhat surprised by her own change in attitude.

Carrie: "After taking EDU 330, my ideas of math have changed. To be quite honest, I was not looking forward to this class at all! Now that I am just about finished with it, I realize that positive feelings can exist in the math classroom! ...For example, the idea behind fractions puzzled me during my elementary/junior high years. They seem so frightening that some kids give up before they even start. Using the Cuisenaire Rods can bring an ease of understanding into what sometimes can be a very confusing topic."

The following quote from Michelle shows that the need for making mathematics meaningful to these students is very real.

Michelle: "I learned [in EDU 330] that math can be learned visually and materially with hands-on learning and it's not all just abstract principles that are hard to understand. I learned that there can actually be meaning behind all the numbers and symbols in mathematics. Also, because of the Christian background of the school, I found out that God gave us the understanding and reasoning of math for a purpose, and because of that understanding, we are able to think more logically about the world"

Heather comment reveals that the course has benefit even for
students who do not bring negative attitudes or mathematical defi-
ciencies with them into the course.

Heather: "Mathematics has enlarged its boundaries in my mind
throughout this semester. Before taking this class, my view of
mathematics included only problems solved by some use of
numbers. Positive past experiences from math classes involved
both my ability to receive high grades and the enjoyment I
obtained from discovering solutions, while negative memories
revolved around my frustration with story problems, especially
in calculus. Because of so many of the activities we engaged in
this semester, I have had to broaden my view of mathematics.
I certainly would never have thought I would be writing papers
for math class! Previously, grammar and math were totally
unrelated for me."

Also from Heather is an insight into the benefits of a Christian
perspective.

Heather: "Math is not limited to problem solving; it is the
continuous endeavor to discover God's set order in all of
creation. That is how I want my future math students to view
mathematics."

The Mathematical Topics

An emphasis is placed on geometry and spatial reasoning. Part of
the reason for this is that research shows that this is an area in which
many elementary teachers are weak. Another reason is that this topic
provides an entry into the content of mathematics that can be
surprisingly pleasant for the students. We work with tangram pieces,
geoboards, Cuisenaire Rods, and pattern blocks. One of the more
fruitful investigations involves tessellations with three-color
combinations from the pattern blocks. This activity involves
combinatorics, geometry, spatial reasoning, and aesthetics.

A second area of emphasis is the base-ten number system. Because
the foundations of our number system are so elegant, it is often
mistakenly assumed that the number system is simple. Students use
chip trading activities to explore how our number system operates. Base
four is used as an alternative base to help students gain insight into the
ordinary base 10 system.

Many of the activities provide students with opportunities to form connections between and among fractions, decimals, percents, ratio, and proportion. We use Cuisenaire Rods, base-ten blocks, tangram pieces, grid paper, and various kinds of dot paper to investigate these topics.

The most sophisticated topics studied are probability and linear functions expressed algebraically and graphically. These topics are found in many of today's elementary mathematics textbooks. However, they were rarely included in elementary curricula ten to fifteen years ago when most of these students were in elementary school.

The Journals

One of the more innovative components of the course is the production of journals. Beginning in the first week of the course students work in groups to develop a sort of professional journal on the learning of mathematics. Each of these journals will have its own unique content focus, which grows from a policy statement constructed by the students during the early part of the semester.

Why Include Writing?

In a constructivist mathematics classroom the communication of mathematical ideas is of great importance. Although most of this communication takes place through speaking and listening, there is an added dimension that occurs as learners write about mathematics. When a learner succeeds in making a mathematical discovery or construction it may be initially very difficult to articulate the concept to another person. The very process of writing causes the learner to think more deeply and more precisely about what he or she has discovered. This process of thinking deeply and precisely actually refines the learner's understanding of the mathematical concept itself.

How Is The Writing Project Organized?

The first task of each group is to develop a written policy statement identifying the goals and vision of the group. This statement is used by the rest of the students throughout the semester as they generate their papers and submit them for publication. The students are given several short writing assignments related to the investigations that they are conducting in class. A typical assignment asks them to determine all of the three-color combinations that can be made from their sets of pattern blocks and then write about the process that they used to ensure that they had obtained *all* of the possible three-color combinations. (A set of pattern blocks has six different geometric shapes, each of which is a unique color.) The essays that the students write in response to these assignments are graded and returned, at which point they may be submitted to one of the boards for publication. In addition to the assigned writings, the students are given a list of suggested topics on which they may choose to write. Many students write on topics that are not assigned or suggested; they invent their own topics based on their own interests. Each student is required to submit at least one paper to each of the boards except for the board of which he or she is a member.

As papers are submitted to the boards the boards meet together to discuss and make decisions about publication of the papers. (Fifteen to twenty minutes of class time is devoted to these meetings each day of class.) The boards compare the papers to their stated policies and make judgments about the quality and suitability of each submitted article. Boards decide to accept papers, request revisions, or reject papers on the basis of criteria that are established in the policy statements.

Often in the discussion of papers, boards discover that their policy statements contain some ambiguities or vagueness. When this happens they need to decide whether to refine their policy statement or live with it as it is. If a refinement is made, then they need to announce any changes to the class so that the authors can adjust to the changes.

Near the end of the semester a deadline is set by which all first drafts must be submitted. Following that deadline the boards meet intensively to finalize their selections and to assemble their journal. They must make decisions about organizational schemes, themes, presentation details, and aesthetics. One week before the scheduled date for the final exam each journal must be turned in for its grade. At that point I sequester myself for several days and read and grade the journals. Instead of a final exam, we gather together for one more time for a "publication" party. At this point, copies of all the journals are made available to all the students, and I share with the group my reactions to each of the journals. Students are charged a fee to cover the duplicating costs, and each student keeps a copy of each journal.

What Are The written Products?

The journals that were produced the last Fall are available for inspection. The themes of the journals ranged from introspective examination of mathematical learning, to classroom ideas for teaching math, to practical applications of math in the "real world." I was quite literally astonished at the high quality of most of the work. It was much more thoughtfully done than I had expected it to be.

Teaching Elementary Mathematics

Field-Based Assignments

Our EDU 331, Teaching of Elementary Mathematics, is a field-based course. It is one of four courses that are integrated into what we call our Advanced Field Experience Block. The students spend all day Tuesday in class and all day Thursday in one of the local schools. The course text (Schwartz & Riedesel, 1994) is designed for use in field-based courses, and it supports the philosophical orientation that has been developed through EDU 330. We require specific assignments that make use of the field placement. In the mathematics component there are four assignments. The first is an analysis/evaluation of three different math texts. The second is that the students must teach a math game. The third is that they must teach a math lesson using the problem-focused lesson template. The fourth is a term assignment involving the use of math manipulatives.

For this fourth assignment the students are placed into groups and each group is given a class set of some manipulative. Their goal is to "become experts in the use of this manipulative" and then report to the group on what they found. It is expected that becoming experts will involve taking every opportunity to use the manipulatives in the classroom.

Reflects On The Previous Course

Where the course in elementary mathematics was primarily concerned with mathematical content, this course is primarily concerned with mathematics pedagogy. It is in this course that the reflective nature of the entire experience is revealed. In this course attention is placed on the pedagogical techniques that were used to teach mathematics in the first course. For example, in the first course the students were repeatedly presented with lessons structured around the problem-focused lesson template. In this course that template is made an explicit object of study, and the students are expected to create their own lessons based on it.

The Problem-Focused Lesson Template

I	Pose a realistic problem that can be solved using the math you intend to teach.

II	Give kids time in small groups (or individually) to solve the problem in whatever way makes sense to them.

- As some groups or individuals find a solution, challenge them to find another way to solve the problem.

- As some groups or individuals find an alternative solution, challenge them to find as many ways as possible to solve the problem.

III	(The previous two indented steps take place while everyone else is finding one way to solve the problem.)

III	Bring the class together as a whole group to share their various ways of solving.

IV	After a period of time in which they communicate together about their solutions, present *another* way of solving the problem. Your new way (if it hasn't come from the children themselves) will make use of the mathematics that you are intending to teach.

Use Of Manipulative Kits And Journals

One of the benefits of having these two courses structured in the way that they are is that the materials used and produced in the first course become resources for the students to use in their field experience of the second course. The manipulatives in the kits are available for use with individual students and with small groups. If the students are willing to share their resources, they can assemble a class set of any of the materials in the kits. Many students have reported that they have used the manipulatives in one-on-one tutoring situations, even though this has not been specifically assigned.

Replication

Professors wishing to replicate the experience we provide should strongly consider adopting the major design elements of the course in mathematics for elementary teachers. The philosophical/historical introduction provides a Christian perspective. The investigative nature of the course helps students experience math in a new way, and this helps them to overcome harmful attitudes. The production of journals helps them deepen their understanding of math as they create articles and as they respond evaluatively to one another's articles. This combination of experiences helps the students to strengthen their content understanding in the area of mathematics while at the same time developing helpful beliefs and attitudes about the teaching of mathematics.

A final quote from one of the students, Alyce, serves as a summary of the goals that are being achieved through this experience.

• Looking back over the semester, I can now say that I'm glad I took Education 330. Not only am I leaving the class with some great ideas packaged nicely in a handy, blue bag, but also with a new attitude about mathematics.

• For me mathematics is no longer only needed for college but is now all around me just waiting for me to discover. I am now more excited about mathematics. I actually enjoy class and look forward to it.

• I know, too, that I am not as deficient in math as I previously believed. I may not find the answer to a problem the same way as a classmate has, but, that is acceptable. God created all of us to be different, yet equal, meaning we can find the answer to the same problem differently.

References

Ediger, M. (1992). The philosophical arena and reading. Reading Improvement, 29(1), 70-74.

Ernest, P. (1989). The knowledge, beliefs and attitudes of the mathematics teacher: A model. Journal of Education for Teaching, 15(1), 13-33.

Narode, R. B. (1987). Constructivism in math and science education. No. ED 290 616).

National Council of Teachers of Mathematics (1989). Curriculum and evaluation standards for school mathematics. Reston, VA: National Council of Teachers of Mathematics.

Schwartz, J. E. (1992) An analysis of mathematics teaching reform orientation focusing on teachers' beliefs and mathematics understanding. Unpublished Doctoral Dissertation, State University of New York at Buffalo.

Schwartz, J. E., & Riedesel, C. A. (1994). Essentials of classroom teaching: Elementary mathematics. Boston: Allyn and Bacon.

Chapter 4

Imaging God and Effectively Preparing ReadingTeachers as Reflective Practitioners

James K. Rooks
Redeemer College, Ancaster, Ontario

The gist of this chapter will speak favourably about reflective teaching, but, I need to get a few questions out in the open first. The literature about teacher reflection, and perhaps our thinking as well, is vague and not focused. Trying to define teacher reflection for a colleague not involved in teacher education made me realize how this is a somewhat unassailable idea? My colleague's assessment was simply: "But isn't that what all good teachers have always done?"

Reflective teaching can be conceived of in so many different ways and mean so many different things that it means very little. According to Zeichner, "There is not a single teacher educator who would say that he or she is not concerned about preparing teachers who are reflective." (Zeichner and Tabachnick 1991, 1)   Nor, I might add, a single Christian college teacher educator who does not feel at least slightly uneasy about linking teacher education with the latest fad in secular education. Yet we recognise that naming a new idea in education as too vague or just a fad is not a responsible alternative to giving it careful consideration and evaluation (Van Dyk 1994). Al Wolters in Creation Regained puts it this way: "It is the task of every educator to sift out the valuable insights of a tradition and make them fruitful for further progress as well as to expose and reject the falsehood and illusion within that same tradition" (1985, 79).

We might also worry that teacher reflection could be part of our society's obsession with always improving, never being quite good enough, or perhaps even a form of works righteousness. A criticism that deserves more consideration comes from noting the lineage of this reflective teacher movement: If not the parents of teacher reflection, persons like Giroux, Pinar, Apple, and Freire, (names I see in the teacher reflection literature) are at least in the teacher reflection family. The Neo-Marxist critique of schooling which they represent, although admittedly insightful at times, certainly serves a different master than we wish to serve (VanBrummelen 1988).

A last concern of mine is the openness to new forms of knowledge that teacher reflection speaks of: Does this post-modern critique provide a meaningful openness, or is it a new form of dogmatism which says the only true knowledge is personal knowledge, and that empirical research has nothing to say about how children learn and how we should teach? I fear this possibility the most since the field of reading education has been highly polarized ever since Rudolph Flesch gave his strongly worded assessment of Why Johnny Can't Read. Ken Goodman and Frank Smith continue the polemic and have come to personify the dogmatic position in their out- of-hand dismissal of any experimental findings which contradict their firmly held opinions (Adams 1991).

Despite these misgivings, I embrace teacher reflection. And to my colleague who says, "But haven't good teachers always been reflective about what they are doing?" I say "Exactly!" What we have intuitively known about good teaching--that it is inherently reflective--we must consciously work toward in the design of teacher education programs.

While teacher reflection is not something new under the sun, it does represent a major shift in emphasis in teacher education (Valli 1992). As Doug Blomberg notes in his chapter in this volume, we need to recognise the complex, dynamic and contextual nature of teaching.

Educating reflective Christian teachers is about shaping our teacher education programs, our teaching, and our interactions with our students in order to help them be discerning teachers, and we must embrace it. Christians are called to be consciously and constantly reforming their goals and their methods in obedient service to their God. In preparing teachers, our task as teacher educators is to help our students recognise the complexity of teaching and the need for informed, intelligent decisions. We must affirm in Christian teacher education programs the need for our students to develop "the knowledge, disposition and analytic skills needed to make good decisions." (Valli 1992, xii)

Having talked briefly about reflection and teacher education, let me now focus specifically on the teaching of reading. As a professor of reading education, I support reflective teaching for two reasons: one, I believe it supports a view of teachers that is in harmony with the biblical account of who we are as God's image bearers; and two, effective reading instruction requires a form of reflective teaching. The first reason is confessional; the second, practical.

The recent monograph by Bette Bosma and Kathryn Blok (1992), A Christian Approach to Teaching Reading, supports my first point in its clear articulation of teachers as images of God:

> To be a person created in God's image means to be able to make decisions, to set goals, and to move in the direction of those goals.... In a curricular area as problematic as the teaching of reading, it is important that in preparing to become a teacher, one accepts the decisional nature of Christ's image within oneself. (1992, 20)

> And in paraphrasing Kuitert they say that being "...an image bearer is not to be viewed as a still-life picture but as a reflection of God in concrete actions." (1992, 21)

These quotes reflect characteristics of a biblical view of the teacher. Reading teachers are called to reflect God in their role in the classroom, analyzing the abilities and understandings of their students alongside what they, as teachers, know about reading. The teacher reflects God's image in making decisions about what and how to teach reading to their students. We need reflective, adaptive reading teachers, then, because that is how teachers can obediently image their Creator in their work in the classroom. God calls teachers to work in this way with their students.

Teachers as decision makers is a key aspect of reflective teaching. It moves us away from a technical/rational model of teaching and toward an affirmation of the richness of God's creation and the complexity of human learning. Teacher proof materials, in this view of teaching, are antithetical to reflective teaching of reading.

Thus, I support reflective teaching on confessional grounds. The second reason for my support is a more practical one: reflective teaching is the best way to ensure that all students learn to read. In order to have effective reading instruction, we must have teachers who are able and willing to reflect on their actions in the classroom and make intelligent, informed decisions about how best to teach their students to read. Effective reading instruction cannot take place without a clear knowledge of basic reading processes, a keen sense of the developmental principles of early reading acquisition, and a careful assessment of the students' abilities. Good reading teachers must possess this knowledge of students and subject in order to teach reading effectively.

Unfortunately, according to reading research, much instruction is not based on a clear knowledge of the reading process and students' academic needs. Reports on classroom practice show the prevalence of all that is antithetical to reflective teaching: an activity-focused, unreflective following of basal reading programs which are unresponsive to students' literacy needs. Shefelbine and Shiel's summation is quite grim: "Researchers who have studied classroom reading instruction have described teachers as technicians who have abdicated instructional decision making to basal texts and their affiliated workbooks" and the picture is one of "teachers concentrating on activities rather than on instructional objectives and students' needs." (1990, 30)

At-risk students, the weak readers, need reflective reading teachers if they are to avoid failure. It is becoming increasingly clear that the activity-focused, unreflective teaching of reading described by Shefelbine and Shiel is very harmful especially for the at-risk students--those students who enter school with a weak literacy background. It is the at-risk students, the weak readers, who become the victims of unreflective instruction. Marilyn Adams has focused attention on the critical discrepancy between the significant number of students who enter school with 1000 or more hours of literacy experiences, well prepared to understand and benefit from almost any type of reading instruction, and the substantial number of students who encounter grade one reading instruction with little or no prior exposure to print (1990). Students with weak backgrounds need clear and appropriate instruction at their level and at their pace if they are going to learn to read; these students need reflective reading teachers.

Students who do not get such appropriate instruction in the early grades fall further and further behind their classmates: "The Matthew Effect," with good readers getting richer (in vocabulary, fluency, and comprehension) while weak readers get poorer (Stanovich 1986). Allington in his 1983 study estimated that good readers in grade two read ten times as many words as the poor readers. Clearly, it is important that students learn to read early on in their schooling. The importance of effective reading instruction in the early grades is further attested to by the research which indicates the probability is very high that a weak reader at the end of grade one will be a weak reader at the end of grade four (Juel 1988).

Having sought to establish that Christian teachers are called to be reflective teachers of reading, imaging God and focusing their instruction on the particular literacy needs of their students, in the final portion of this paper I will deal specifically with our situation as teacher educators. Peek into a grade three classroom; you may see a group of four or five students sitting in a circle with their teacher; each one has the basal reader open on their laps and they are taking turns reading a sentence or a paragraph aloud. When a student reads haltingly the other students jump in to correct him or her or to supply a word which the reader is struggling to decipher. This is a picture of the weak reader group in the classroom. We know from studies that this group will do quite a bit of oral reading and not all that much silent reading. We know that they will cover substantially less material than the other groups. We also know, from the monograph Becoming a Nation of Readers, that this scenario is all too prevalent in our classrooms and that there is a strong pattern of inferior instruction for the students in these weak reader groups (Anderson 1985).

The particular practice of a group of students reading aloud is called round robin reading. It has been discredited by research and widely discouraged in teacher education programs for at least the last twenty years. The continuing widespread use of round robin reading despite the indictment of research and teacher training illustrates the need for reflective teachers who are able to examine traditional practices. Reflective teacher education seeks to encourage teachers to examine their own practices and the commonly accepted practices in their school in light of what they know about reading and what their students need to learn.

Susan Adler says that "The best teachers are researchers, able to systematically reflect on their own teaching" (Adler 1993, 160). Doug Blomberg, while preferring the metaphor of teachers as "articulate artisans", agrees that teachers must examine their own teaching practices (this volume). To what extent do the teacher graduates from Christian colleges leave our programs prepared to systematically reflect on their own teaching and be articulate artisans? To what extent can I, as a teacher educator, help my students image God and be effective teachers of reading in their critical first years of teaching? Let me share some of my observations of student teachers and beginning teachers, as well as raise a few related questions about our role as teacher educators in helping our students to become reflective teachers.

These scenes are drawn from my research into my own practice where I am attempting to be a reflective teacher of reading education.

Observation #1

Ann is working in a five week placement teaching grade one. She had taken my course on teaching reading last semester, and now I am observing her student teaching during the scheduled phonics lesson for her class. I watch for twenty-five minutes as she has the grade one children come to the front in groups of five with each child in the group holding up a picture. The students in their seats are asked to correctly sequence the pictures being held up by their classmates. Ann says: "Okay, which one of these pictured activities comes first? Right, the picture of the sun rising shows us it is morning, and then the picture of the children eating breakfast and getting ready for school comes next." The class proceeds by identifying the picture of the children on their way to school next, then the picture showing dusk, and then a last one of the darkness. The students have put the pictures in the correct sequence.

The twenty-five minutes pass as each group comes to the front while students in their seats help sequence the pictures; the bell rings as the last group stands at the front. Ann tells the children to turn to page eighty-nine and to quickly put the pictures on that page in order. The task requires the students to sequence two groups of four pictures, putting number "one" on the first one, number "two" on the second...etc.. The students complete this very quickly and everyone heads out for recess within a minute or two.

Ann and I meet to discuss the lesson. Our conversation goes something like this:

J.R.: Okay let's talk about your lesson today. Tell me about it.

Ann: Well, I think it went okay. The kids got mixed up with a few pictures.

J.R: Okay, well, where did this idea come from? Why were you doing this?

Ann: I thought it up myself.

J R.: It was your idea, then? It was your lesson to choose what to do?

Ann: No, the teacher just told me to do the next phonics workbook page, so this is what I came up with.

Ann seemed to have no problem with the lesson and its conception; she was satisfied with the goal of teaching sequencing. When I reluctantly concluded that I was going to have to be the one to point out that the relationship between the lesson and the children learning to read was very weak at best, Ann responded as if I did not understand the situation: "This was not supposed to be a reading lesson; they do that at another time during the day. This was the phonics lesson."

I do not blame Ann for the narrow scope of this lesson, and I do not wish to criticize her for failing to critique the objective given by her supervising teacher; I am trying to understand the situation that student teachers like Ann find themselves in and what this has to say about how and what I seek to teach in pre-service education courses. All of the students in my teaching of reading class, of which Ann was one, had concluded that there is not "one best way to teach reading." We came to the position where we were neither stridently opposed to phonics nor adamantly set against whole language: we read Adams (1990), Anderson (1985), and Stahl (1992) on the nature of good phonics instruction and how ineffective phonics workbooks were. We agreed that phonics instruction should be done for only one reason and with one purpose in mind: helping students learn to read for meaning and comprehension.

That Ann would be having a separate phonics time block and reading time block does not surprise me or disturb me. Nor do I find it surprising that Ann had a difficult time understanding what she was really supposed to do with the instruction from her supervising teacher: "Do the next page in the phonics workbook." Yet, I am brought up short by the realization that the understanding she previously articulated about teaching reading seemed to have no place in her consciousness as she prepared to teach this phonics lesson or in our discussion following the lesson.

This picture of Ann is a very far cry from the picture of a reflective teacher bringing to bear her knowledge of the principles of reading acquisition and the needs of her particular students to shape instruction that is clearly directed and effective.

The visit with Ann offered me no evidence that my course in teaching reading had accomplished the objective Lee Shulman holds out for us as teacher educators in his paraphrase of Fenstermacher: "The goal of teacher education ... is not to indoctrinate or train teachers to behave in prescribed ways, but to educate teachers to reason soundly about their teaching as well as to perform skilfully." (1987, 13) Was it only an inadequate teacher supervisor that caused this situation or some trait of the student teacher herself? Or was it the power of the commercially produced curriculum that needed "to be covered?" Or was it perhaps a missing component in her teaching of reading course which would have helped her understand the limited potential of the ubiquitous phonics workbooks with their focus on the rules and sub-skills of reading?

Observation #2

The scenario with Ann closely parallels my earlier experience with Leslie, a beginning teacher with whom I worked over the course of several months. When I came in to observe Leslie's language arts program, she was floating along covering a story from the grade four reader every second day or so, following up the reading of the story with an activity chosen from the teacher's guide and a page or two from the students' activity book. Despite using a program that purports to be a whole language approach with a focus on real literature to be read for meaning, I noted that the students did not see themselves as engaged in real reading and writing, and they perceived that Leslie had no clear sense of direction in her program.

As part of our work together, Leslie began to keep a journal, writing three times a week. Clearly, writing can be a good way to foster reflection, but it is no panacea. In Leslie's case it was not helping her be reflective in a broad or deep way. It was only after we had been working together for about six weeks and she happened to reread her journal from her teacher education program that she could see that she had narrowed the scope of her writing and thinking to the students' behaviour, or rather misbehaviour. Her journal recorded a good lesson if the students behaved reasonably well, and a failure if they misbehaved.

In her teacher education program, she commented, her journal writing had been much more diverse and perceptive. It seemed that Leslie's reflection as a teacher was blocked partially by the over-whelming problem of managing 24 grade four students. Leslie's discovery of her narrow focus as a first year teacher did not change everything for her, but it is worth noting that one result of her going back to her college notes on the teaching of reading was her recollection and subsequent teaching of a terrific lesson with a strong focus and clear goal.

Leslie's experience shows that beginning teachers can be reflective and remember their ideals and their understandings which they developed in their teacher education programs. What would help teachers get in touch with what they know and believe in the face of the demands of day-to-day teaching? Although we cannot expect all of our students to remember all of what we seek to teach them, we as teacher educators need to ask what we can do to foster reflective teacher educators who take that reflective orientation into their teaching. To be useful and applicable, John Van Dyke reminds us, new knowledge must be learned in situations that make it applicable to concrete problem-solving (1993).

Observation #3

Some problems arise from the constraints of the particular school and its prescriptive curriculum. Doug graduated last year from the college where I teach; he is now teaching in a Christian school in the Toronto area. Doug is a creative person who believes strongly in the importance of a literacy rich environment; he wants the school day to be filled with meaningful reading and writing.

Yet, when I visited Doug he said that he is providing fewer and fewer of these literacy experiences he believes are needed by his students. He is worried about his students not doing well on the regular round of standardized tests which he is required to administer and report on. He surmises that their poor test results stem from his failure to cover enough of the pages in the three language workbooks his students must use.

He knows that the time he spends on meaningful reading and writing activities are extremely helpful for his students and he sees his students making good progress in learning to read, write, and spell. The tests, however, do not pick up their progress in those areas; they assess the student's ability to recall the particular rules taught in the highly prescriptive program.

It is not difficult to understanding why Doug's practice is not reflecting the knowledge and beliefs he developed in his teacher education program. It is difficult to know how to help Doug be a reflective teacher of reading in his particular situation.

Observation #4

And then we have Betty; her experience can be held up as the ideal. After student teaching in grade one with a teacher supervisor who has a strong, clear focus and commitment to ensuring all of her children to read, Betty was hired to come back and teach grade one across the hall from her former supervisor. Now she is using and adapting a curriculum she is familiar with and setting up her program in a somewhat similar fashion to her mentor. She is keenly focused on her grade one students' abilities: in the first week of September she notices that a few of her students are not understanding her instruction in reading class and she is

60   Nurturing Reflective Christians To Teach

going to have to back up and first help them understand what a word is.
By early October, Betty can tell you who the weak readers in her room
are and what she is doing to keep them motivated to learn to read. She
has found ways to focus her instruction on their particular needs.

Is Betty's situation just a fortunate occurrence, a fortuitous coming
together of all the right conditions to create a possibility for Betty to be
a reflective, decision-making, God-imaging, effective first year teacher
of reading? Is it something about Betty that made her this kind of
reflective teacher? Or is it the positive role model she had for a
supervising teacher?

Does Betty's situation suggest a direction for shaping student
teaching? Should all student teachers be working with someone like
Betty's supervising teacher at some point? Should first year teachers be
matched up with a mentor who will help them be reflective and focused
in their first year of teaching?

The unanswered questions are numerous, but the goal is clear: we,
as Christian teacher-educators, need to help our students be reflective in
their teacher education courses, their student teaching, and their first
years of teaching. We need to keep looking for answers to the
questions: What hinders the development of reflective teaching? What
can be done to foster good reflective teaching. We need, in the words of
Bette Bosma and Kathryn Blok, to help teachers to focus on the
questions: "What is the child ready to learn that I should teach?" and
"How can I change my teaching behaviour to provide this learner with
daily success experiences?"

We need to fulfil our calling as teacher educators by helping our
students fulfil their calling from God as teachers who image God in the
classroom.

Bibliography

Adams, M. J. 1990. Beginning to Read: Thinking and Learning
     About... Print. Cambridge. MA: MIT Press.

Adams, M. J. 1991. Why not phonics and whole language? In All
     Language and the Creation of Literacy. ed. W. Ellis,
     Baltimore, MD: Orton Dyslexia Society.

Adler, S. 1993. Teacher education: Research as reflective practice.
     Teacher & Teacher Education. 9(2): 159-167.

Anderson, R. & E. Hiebert, J. Scott A. Wilkinson 1985. Becoming a Nation of Readers: The report of the commission on reading. Washington D.C. National Institute of Education.

Allington R. L. 1983. The reading instruction provided readers of differing reading ability. Elementary School Journal 83: 549-559.

Bosma, B. and K. Blok 1992. A Christian perspective on the teaching of reading. Grand Rapids, Mich.: Calvin College Monograph.

Christensen, C. & D. Garvin, A. Sweet eds. 1991. Education for Judgment: The Artistry of Discussion Leadership. Boston, MA: Harvard Business School Press.

Juel, C. 1988. The early detection of reading difficulties. (3rd ed.). Portsmouth, NH: Heineman.

Postman, N. 1979. Teaching as a conserving activity. New York: Dell.

Shefelbine J. & G. Shiel 1990. Preservice teacher's schemata for a diagnostic framework in reading. Reading Research and Instruction. 30(1): 30-43

Shulman, L.S. 1987. Knowledge and teaching: Foundations of the new reform. Harvard Educational Review. 57(1): 1-22.

Stahl, S. A. 1992. Saying the "p" word:Nine guidelines for exemplary phonics instruction. The Reading Teacher 45(8): 1 625.

Stanovich, K. 1986. Matthew effects in reading :Some consequences of individual differences in the acquisition of literacy. Reading Research Quarterly. 21: 360-407.

Valli, L. 1992 ed. Reflective teacher education: Cases and critiques. Albany, NY: State University of New York Press.

Van Brummelen, H. 1988. Becoming "born again"--the Marxist way. Christian Educators Journal. 27(4): 6-7.

Van Dyk J. 1993 Improving teaching and learning. Pro Rege. 21(4): 3-35.

Van Dyk J. 1994. Can Christian schools change? Christian Educators Journal. 33(3): 4-5.

Wolters, A. 1985. Creation regained: Biblical basics for a reformational worldview. Grand Rapids: Eerdmans.

Zeichner, K. M. 1991. Reflections on reflective teaching. In Issues and practices inquiry-oriented teacher education. eds. K.M. Zeichner & B. R. Tabachnick, London: Falmer Press.

Chapter 5

Reflection On Exceptionality: Toward An Inclusive World View

Ken A. Pudlas
Trinity Western University
Langley, British Columbia, Canada

Introduction And Rationale

This paper is born out of the union of two apparently disparate yet related topics. The first comes from the question which is at the foundation of this conference, "How do we as Christian professors of education shape our foundations and methods courses to encourage teachers to be change agents in education?". The second is the fact that teachers in all types of schools and at all levels are increasingly likely to encounter exceptional students who require special education. Thus it is important to explore the necessity of and the methodology for enabling teachers to become agents of change in dealing with students who have special needs. It would be prudent at this point to define some of the terminology (in the event that any participants may be unfamiliar with the field).

Definition of Terms

It has been suggested that deviancy is in the eye of the beholder (Wolfensberger, 1972). Thus each of us present could at some point be considered "deviant" or exceptional. This point is nicely illustrated by the "Animal Crackers" cartoon, in which a toad with "huge bulbous eyes, and a big wide mouth, and a wonderfully even distribution of warts all over her body..." is referred to as "...a classic beauty!". Of course, this observation is made by another toad.

Certainly when God is the beholder, each of us has fallen short of His ultimate standard, and thus could be considered deviant. Specific to the topic at hand, however, an exceptional student differs from the average or normal child in: mental characteristics, sensory abilities, commu-nication abilities, behavior and emotional development, and or physical characteristics to such a degree that they require special education in order to meet their full potential. Special education, as part of these circular definitions, refers to the educational modifications or help devised for children who differ significantly from the norm. These modifications may be academic or environmental.

One of the reasons that teachers are likely to encounter exceptional students is the move in public schools toward an inclusive model, wherein all students, regardless of any disability, are educated in regular classrooms by regular teachers. Special education is not new, nor is the practice of integration. However, the full inclusion now extant does give rise to unique problems for today's teachers, many of whom may not have had any previous education or training in exceptionality. Some of these are explored in an article by Fuchs and Fuchs (1994). They suggest that, "...the field's rhetoric has become increasingly strident and its perspective increasingly insular and disassociated from general education's concerns" (p. 294). They conclude by suggesting that solutions may come from inventive pragmatists rather than extremists on the right or left. Perhaps those of us involved in preparing reflective Christian practitioners can be a part of the solution.

Many participants at this conference will have offered their definitions of "reflection". Long before the current popularity of the term, Dewey (1904) suggested that it is more important to make teachers thoughtful, alert students of education than it is to help them gain immediate job proficiency. Preprofessional teachers need to have inculcated within them the importance of lifelong learning; for Christian teachers that involves the continual evolution of their biblical worldview. Distilled to its essence the term reflection, as used in this paper, will be taken to mean simply "asking questions of oneself". As

Cruickshank suggested, it is of primary importance that reflection on teaching begin early in preservice preparation and that it be nurtured throughout its duration and beyond (1991, p. 1). Clearly then, students must learn what kinds of questions to ask. One such question is, "What is my view of exceptional persons, and why should they be of concern to me?", and we are thus brought back to the purpose of this paper: developing personally, (and, through modeling, in our students) a biblical worldview which includes reflection on exceptionality. As Wolterstorff (1984, p. 9) has suggested, "A person's worldview is their way of thinking about life and the world, coupled with values they set for themselves in the context of that way of thinking".

Reasons For An Inclusive Worldview

As previously noted, inclusion of exceptional students into regular classes has become the norm in public school settings. Both American laws (such as PL 94-142) and Canadian laws serve to protect the right of all students to an appropriate education. In fact, Canadian educational policy concerning students with disabilities is undergoing a paradigmatic shift toward what is often termed the "minority rights paradigm"; a shift from a perspective of charity and exclusion to one of rights and inclusion.

In addition to legal mandates, there is also a moral mandate. For example, Wolterstorff (1984) has suggested that a society can better be judged by how it treats its weak not its strong. This point is illustrated by a cartoon from Whatever Happened to the Human Race?, by Schaefer and Koop wherein two hospital patients are shown in their beds, attached to numerous tubes, and in full view of the headline reading "Some favor pulling plug on terminally ill", one patient turns to the other and says, "Watch my plugs, will you, I'm going to take a nap". While the wry humor may bring a smile, a quick perusal of the news will indicate that abortion and euthanasia are very real issues in today's society. Most thinking Christians are outraged at the prospect of taking a life. However, as Helen Keller suggested, it is not enough to give the handicapped life, they must be given a life worth living.

We are also given a biblical mandate (see for example Matthew 18, or, in II Samuel 9, the story of David and Mephibosheth) not to neglect those who may be deemed weaker. Further, in terms of our Christian identity as described in I John (see for example, 3:11,16; 4:7,8) we are to be characterized by love. This is not an "exclusionary" policy, wherein we can love only the lovely, but rather it is one of inclusion.

Dangers Inherent In Inclusion

In spite of the theoretical defensibility of the inclusive movement in education (or its predecessors, variously named as integration, the Regular Education Initiative, or Zero Reject), it may be placing both teachers and students at risk (see for example, Pudlas, 1993). In order to illustrate the nature of the risk, and to move from an esoteric to a more pragmatic level, an excerpt from a letter written by the mother of a teenager is included.

> He was the happiest most well adjusted pre-schooler and toddler that any mother could wish for. We were told by the specialist when he was eighteen months old that there would be many things that he would never be able to do because he   had cerebral palsy. Not so!   He accomplished everything the said was impossible without fear, tension, or stress before he started school.
>
> I should point out that his handicap was not very severe, to look at him you would not know there was a problem, it was mostly his fine motor movements and speech that was affected. "Bob" started school as a well-adjusted child and was mainstreamed into kindergarten. It was not long before Bob's teacher informed us that his speech was not good enough for regular class and he was segregated into a class at a school many miles from home which dealt with children with speech problems. This was after she failed him. He stayed in segregated classes until grade four, by which time he had been taught to speak clearly, was up-to-date on all school work and was so very excited about going back to a regular class. What a shock he was in for! He began to change into an argumentative defensive child at home... He was the butt of every cruel and vindictive child in elementary school... He was on the outside looking in... His nose was flicked by those same peers over several months during class and play until the side of his nose split from his face. His teachers never saw any of this. They were too busy. He begged me not to say anything as if he or I said something then he would be hurt more or nobody would like him... Bob never became a behavior problem at school. His frustrations were bottled up until he got home from school, and then he would explode...
>
> I love my son dearly, but if the need arose, I would never put another child through the misery he has endured. **Mainstreaming may be the answer, but it destroyed the love and laughter in my little boy's face.** (Emphasis added).

Granted, as the empirical purist would quickly point out, this is only one anecdotal report. It is, nevertheless an actual case, and it does illustrate two important areas of risk: (1) the risk of peer rejection, and; (2) the risk of inefficacy of regular class teachers.

Just what is the nature and purpose of special education; are we losing sight of the original goals in an attempt to "do the right thing", and; as Christian educators, ought our biblical worldview affect the nature of the educational experience we offer? Partial answers to these questions may be found in two illustrations which follow. (It is the experience of the author that "lectures" are soon forgotten, but "stories" tend to lodge, at times annoyingly, in the memory).

The first illustration is adapted from a story told by a psychologist of no small repute, James Dobson, although the application is original.

> The story is told of research done with the (invol-untary?) assistance of a walleyed pike. This feisty fish was placed in a large tank and fed fingerlings. When the contented fish was not looking, a clear partition was inserted to separate the two sides of the tank. Food was again placed in the water, and the pike swam toward it, and... yes, banged his nose on the barrier. Not a quitter, it tried repeatedly to reach the goal. After some
> time the barrier was removed. However, the pike was later found "tanning his tummy at the top of the tank".

What was the cause of death? Why had the starvation occurred? More importantly, what is the point? The pike had learned failure; the barrier could not be overcome, and; even when it was removed, the lesson of failure caused by the barrier was not forgotten. The application? The essence of special education is the removal of barriers which may cause academic, or emotional, or social starvation. It is essential therefore, that teachers be aware of the nature of those barriers. Clearly, the teachers in "Bob's" case were not aware of or not equipped to deal with the needs of this exceptional student. Since no teacher would deliberately turn a blind eye to such mistreatment, how could it have occurred?

A second illustration may offer further insights.

> In the not-too-distant past, two hunters drove down a country road in northern British Columbia. In search of moose, they parked their truck at the side of the road, hiked a few hundred yards into the bush, and... BANG! Although they claimed to be inter-ested only in securing meat for their families, this particular animal **did** have trophy sized antlers. As darkness was approaching, each hunter grasped one side of

the antlers and began pulling the recently-deceased toward the road. The thick underbrush caught the out-turned antlers, and impeded progress. One of the hunters (an educator) turned to the other and suggested that they would have an easier time of it if they dragged the animal by its hind legs. This proved to be a much easier way, and after some time, the teacher turned to his companion and said, "Now, isn't this much easier?", to which his companion replied, "Yes, but ... aren't we getting kind of far away from the truck?".

The application? Quite obviously, in taking an apparently easier approach, the hunters had lost sight of their goal. It is possible that in implementing changes in special education, administrators may loose sight of the goal: the removal of barriers which prevent exceptional students from reaching their full potential. Regular classroom teachers, neophytes in special education, may unwittingly place students such as Bob at risk. Why? Because they may be unfamiliar with the unique needs of such students, yet be forced to accept such students because of administrative decisions.

How, then can real or perceived failure be prevented? This is certainly another question that the reflective teacher needs to ask. Another might be, "How likely am I to be faced with such problems?".

Present Status

To this point, the discussion of inclusion has focused on public schools. However, according to the United States Department of Education (1991) nearly one-fourth of all the elementary and secondary schools in the United States are private schools, and 5.2 million school children are enrolled in those schools. According to an article by Sutton, Sutton, and Everett (1993) in the Journal of Research on Christian Education, little was known about the opportunities many private schools provide in the area of special education, particularly among the rapidly growing Christian or fundamentalist schools (p. 66). These authors reported data indicating that less than six percent (5.75%) of these schools were operating a special education program. As disturbing as these results may be, the nature of the special education personnel may be of even greater concern. Results, although taken from a relatively small sample, indicate that often the least experienced and least qualified teachers were involved in providing special education. For example, 75% did not hold teaching certificates from state departments of education or their respective Christian school associations; half had five or fewer years of experience (p. 72).

There is ample reason to believe that the church as a whole may not be fulfilling its mandate. Personal communication with numerous individuals and families indicate that too often, exceptional families or individuals are disappointed by the treatment received at the hands of their fellow Christians. (These persons have expressed these same thoughts in seminars in various classes at Trinity Western University, thereby, hopefully, causing students in those classes to reflect on some of these issues.)

Possible Reasons For Non-Inclusion

Why are Christians too often ineffective in meeting the needs of exceptional persons? A temptingly simple response, especially in light of the theme of this conference, might be that they simply have not included exceptionality in their worldview reflection. Thus their collective ignorance may lead to a natural fear of the unknown. At its extreme, fear of the unknown becomes xenophobia. Perhaps the question has never been explored as to why such individuals, whose birth often causes grief for the families, are even allowed by God to be born, or; if asked, has been answered with the conclusion that disability is the result of sin. This would, after all be a natural conclusion of those who believe that good things happen to good people, and conversely, bad to bad. The idea of "just deserts" would then, in the eyes of some, absolve us from any obligation to come along side. This mind set was demonstrated by the Disciples when they asked Jesus if the blind man or his parents had sinned to cause the blindness (see John 9). Thus we can see that for reflection to be effective, not only must questions be asked, but the correct questions.

Four Key Questions for Reflection

Effective reflection requires the asking of pertinent questions. In this instance, one such question might be, "Is suffering always the result of sin?". If the Genesis creation account is the starting point, then the answer is ultimately yes. This and other questions, though, ought to be part of the preprofessional education of all teachers. Other related questions might include: Does God create all things?; Is God sovereign?; Does God make mistakes?, and; How does a Christian reconcile the fact of exceptionality and attendant human suffering with belief in a loving God?

The four questions pertain to: creation, sovereignty, righteousness, and reconciliation. Clearly these questions are not the exclusive domain of faculties of Education. Other faculties or departments could also initiate thinking regarding exceptional persons within the context of their courses. Philosophy, Religious Studies, Sociology, Anthropology, History, could all include at least a tertiary study of the topic of exceptionality. For example, a philosophy course might deal with ethical issues, one of which would be that of euthanasia and infanticide as related to severely handicapped individuals. In several of her books, Joni Eareckson Tada writes of her deep depression and desire to commit suicide after an accident left her severely disabled; certainly this example of depression could be incorporated into a psychology class. Creative and reflective professors will be able to find many ways to stimulate their students to reflect on the place of exceptional persons in their worldview.

Applications in Christian Colleges and Universities

To illustrate how some of these issues may be addressed, an example of one unit of study from Trinity Western University is offered. All Education majors must take a course entitled "Psychological Foundations of Teaching and Learning". One of the units of study incorporates the "Pudlas Self Esteem Index":

$$SE = \frac{Success}{Aspirations}$$

Four factors considered integral to self esteem are discussed: power, significance, competence, and worth. Students are then challenged to consider the experience of an integrated special needs student in light of these four variables. For example, "significance" refers to a sense of being valued for being alive. Many students with special needs are not made to feel welcome in classrooms where their needs are not understood by either teachers or fellow students. The example of Bob cited above may be all too typical. Another topic in this particular course is that of "Inviting and disinviting classrooms" as defined by Purkey (1984). The discussions in the course concern the means by which all students can be made to feel welcome, and the way in which teachers can structure their classes so as to provide an inviting experience.

Two other courses offered by T.W.U. deal more specifically with the issue of exceptionality. To date, however, these courses are electives, as is the case with special education course work in the other universities in the province. Thus it is possible for education students in British Columbia to graduate and become certified teachers without ever having had any formal special education courses. This might explain, but not excuse, the treatment that Bob received. That is not to say, however, that only education majors should reflect on exceptionality. As previously noted, the topic could and should be discussed in a variety of courses.

Participant Survey

It would be beneficial at this point to be able to discuss what the various institutions represented at this conference currently offer by way of opportunity to reflect on exceptionality. Do state laws currently require special education training? (Perhaps this could be a subject for discussion at subsequent conferences). Do university courses other than education offer opportunities to discuss the issues noted here? Should, for example, various religious studies courses offer "Theology of Exceptionality" as, at the very least, a valid topic for term papers and seminars?

Senior students in a class entitled "Strategies for the Exceptional Student" at Trinity Western University were asked the following question:

"How could your education/understanding of exceptionality be encouraged or enhanced in your courses and experiences at T.W.U.? Give specifics as appropriate."

A sample of their responses include:

"I think if it was discussed more openly in other courses. It seems exceptionality is discussed only in classes such as this where it is the focus. It is important to be **aware** - many students here are not. Providing opportunities whereby students can interact with exceptional students. The panel we had here in class was very informative and really helped to understand more readily where those individuals were coming from. Even in chapel this could be done."

"In a phys. ed. course - maybe Phed 190 have a unit on disabled and how an exercise program for them could be set up. A section in a Rels [Religious Studies] course that deals with our attitude toward the disabled and how God views them."

"Because everyone has to take IDIS 400 [Interdisciplinary Studies] (and 100 level) I would suggest that perhaps someone take a lecture slot and discuss the issue of exceptionality. At one point or another we all will encounter a person of this type. So it wouldn't be a waste of time! (It would be a key lecture). Perhaps offering practical hands on tutoring for LD children making it known to all on campus."

"Have a chance to visit/watch a Special Olympics meet."

Students presented a number of additional insightful and practical suggestions. As a result, some further opportunities to reflect on exceptionality are being planned for the entire Trinity Western University community.

Conclusion

Man's behavior is in good part determined by his ideologies. That is, by a combination of beliefs, attitudes, and interpretations of reality that are derived from experiences, knowledge of what are presumed to be facts, and above all, values (Wolfensberger, 1972). It is important, therefor, that preprofessional education students be given opportunities to rehearse their craft, and to reflect. Encounters with exceptional students and other disabled persons should be a part of that reflection and rehearsal. This will enable the teachers that we graduate to develop an inclusive worldview. When our students come to see exceptional persons as valued by God, they too will come to value those persons. Then exceptional students will naturally be included and enabled to meet their full potential.

References

Cruickshank, D. (1991). Reflective teaching. Bloomington, IN: Phi Delta Kappa.

Fuchs, D., & Fuchs, L. (1994). Inclusive schools movement and radicalization of special education reform. Exceptional Children, 60, (4), 294-309.

Pudlas, K. (1993). Integration: Students and teachers at risk? British Columbia Journal of Special Education, 17, (1), 54-61.

Purkey, W. (1984). Inviting school success: A self-concept approach to teaching and learning. Belmont, CA: Wadsworth Publishing Company.

Sutton, J., Sutton, C., & Everett, E. (1993). Special education in Christian/fundamentalist schools: A commitment to all the children? Journal of Research on Christian Education, 2, (1), 65-79.

Wolfensberger, W. (1972) Normalization: The principle of normalization in human services. Toronto, ON: Leonard Crainford.

Wolterstorff, N. (1984). In Walsh, B. & Middleton, J. The transforming vision: Shaping a Christian worldview. Downers Grove, IL: Intervarsity Press.

Chapter 6

A Quantitative Analysis of Reflective Practice in Preparing Teachers at Christian Colleges

Grant M. Tipton III
& Linda L. Samek
Education Division, Western Baptist College
Salem, Oregon

Introduction

Teaching teachers to teach is not an easy task. Teaching teachers to teach reflectively is even more difficult. Christian teacher educators have a responsibility to prepare teachers whose worldview is somewhat different from that of non-Christian teachers. In carrying out this preparation, it is desired that those teachers will learn not only strategies and course content, but will also develop the ability to consider and/or compose the rationale behind those strategies and course content. In thinking critically about what they do, Christian teachers must be able to ground all their activities in Christian principles.

As the researchers thought about reflective practice and the reflective practitioner, and worked to develop a coherent and concise definition, the discovery was made that although there exists literature that attempts to define reflective practice, very little has been written about who actually teaches the process of reflection, and what practices those teachers believe are important in developing reflective practitioners. Reflective practice is currently an important issue in educational circles. Many educators talk about developing reflective teachers, but most talk in generalities. Do Christian educators, who prepare a portion of the nation's future teachers, believe in reflective practice, and do they put this belief into action by applying those techniques that they think foster reflection in their students? The answers to those questions did not appear to be available in the existing literature.

This being the case, the researchers sought to compile this information through the use of two key questions. In order to facilitate this task, ten practices/techniques were identified that seemed to embody current thinking on what teachers can do to become reflective practitioners. The first question addressed the issue of perceived validity of these practices/techniques by Christian teacher educators. The second question asked these same teacher educators about their own infusion of the ten practices/techniques in their current education courses and their plans for use in future coursework. As a foundation for discussion on infusion of reflective practice in teacher education programs, the researchers believe it is important to understand both belief and actual usage.

In the effort to secure answers to the key questions, the researchers established the following as the objectives for this study:

1. To determine the perception that teacher educators in Christian institutions have concerning various recognized practices and techniques used in attempting to produce reflective preservice teachers.

2. To determine the usage level of various recognized techniques and practices for the infusion of reflection in preservice teachers by teacher educators in Christian institutions.

Review of Literature

Research on reflective practice in education is rather limited in regard to both inservice and preservice teachers. There are many questions and few answers. Ross (1990) suggested that the lack of research may be due, in part, to the fact that reflection is a complex mental process that is difficult to assess. There is not a clear, universally accepted definition of reflective practice, and Ross noted that there may never be such a definition with enough behavioral specificity to measure quantitatively. Zeichner (1987) indicated that most research consists of self-reports or isolated examples of success that may not be generalizable. The research that does exist is, for the most part, qualitative.

The literature relating to reflective practice addresses a number of specific practices/techniques that are infused into teacher education programs to promote reflection in preservice teachers. The practices and techniques which will be considered in this review include: autobiography, case studies, critical inquiry, curriculum analysis and modification, dialoging, ethnography, forums, journals, portfolios, and problematizing.

If teacher educators believe that knowledge is built on prior experience, autobiographies are helpful in thinking about the personal experiences of the student teacher. The students can use autobiographies to explore their own experiences, styles, and goals for teaching (Adler, 1991). Adler believed that autobiographies helped the students move back and forth between experience and the information they were gaining in the teacher education program courses. They can see how personal stories differ and why they differ. The students may also question the unexamined portions of their own lives. Stories are a part of each individual, and to understand happenings in context, an individual will need to make explicit his/her own story.

Case studies are detailed accounts of situations that have or could have happened. They come in various lengths and in a variety of detail. Sparks-Langer et al (1990) determined that adding more case studies to their program afforded their students the opportunity to discuss why things do or do not work. Noordhoff and Kleinfeld (1990) believed that case studies helped their student teachers spot central issues from different viewpoints and consider alternative strategies and predict consequences in a safe environment. Case studies can provide concrete situations for reflection when actual experiences are not possible or have not yet arisen in the student teacher's experience (Adler, 1990). Case studies are most useful in a seminar or small group situation where each student has time to reflect and weigh the alternative solutions to the problem that has been posed.

Adler (1991) suggested that the process of critical inquiry might consist of: (1) writing a narrative of a confusing or perplexing situation, (2) uncovering implicit theories, (3) confronting and re-evaluating operational theories in a broader context, and (4) reconstructing by gaining control of self and considering alternatives. In this process, the reflective teacher has the opportunity to question what is

taken for granted and look for unarticulated assumptions and new perspectives (Adler, 1990).
Curriculum analysis and modification is undertaken to consider what is important for learners and why these things in particular matter (Adler, 1991). Zeichner (1987) stated that curriculum analysis focused on increasing sensitivity to the values and assumptions embedded in particular curriculum materials and programs. Teachers should develop, not just implement, curriculum. In doing this during a teacher education program, a preservice teacher can come to better appreciate the thought that must go into curriculum development. It is important to understand the rationale behind the goals and activities.

Another vital practice or technique, according to Schön (1987), was dialoging. Dialog between student and mentor is necessary for growth and development of the student. The mentor continually prods the student to stretch and grow. Ross (1990) stated that dialoging developed common meaning between the teacher educator and the preservice teacher and encouraged thinking from multiple perspectives. Adler (1990) suggested that dialoging helps the student to more efficiently problematize a situation, which is a necessary step before a problem solving process can be initiated. Dialoging can be between students or between a student and a coach (Adler, 1991).

Zeichner (1987) believed ethnographies to be a valuable tool for developing reflective practitioners. The students were asked to spend time studying and synthesizing systems of classrooms, curriculum, and other facets of the educational process. This assisted the student in discovering hidden assumptions in the organization and then in seeing and inventing alternatives to current practice. Adler (1991) suggested that through a school ethnography a student teacher could systematically discover underlying belief systems and cultures. Before changes can be made, the existing culture of an organization must be understood and accommodated.

Forums are used as a small group process to analyze and solve problems. The students have the opportunity to hear other opinions and may develop the ability to see other perspectives (Adler, 1990) which is an important part of the reflection process. This promotes open-mindedness and a willingness to consider other viewpoints.

Perhaps the most mentioned reflective practice/technique was the journal. Although Zeichner (1987) indicated that there is no clear validation of the efficacy of journal writing for developing reflective practitioners, he did note that, outside the teacher education field, there is documented evidence that journal writing stimulates higher level thinking. Adler (1991) viewed the journal as a valid vehicle for reflection. It is often in journaling that the teacher will make connections in what seem to be ramblings (Canning, 1991). The content of journals varies from program to program. Zeichner (1987) suggested four elements that should be included in a student teacher's journal: what s/he knows, what s/he feels, what s/he does and how it is done, and why s/he does what s/he does. Sparks-Langer et al (1990) included three instructional events for student teachers: what they learned, factors that influenced outcomes, and what they would do differently the next time and why. Frieberg and Waxman (1990) suggested that students record experiences and raise questions in their journals. The instructor then should respond to the journal either verbally or in writing. The literature would seem to indicate that journals are used extensively in the process of developing reflective teachers.

The use of portfolios was not specifically addressed in the literature that was examined by the investigators. However, a portfolio, as defined by the investigators, is a collection of evidence of professional competence. Producing a portfolio requires reflection through self-assessment in order to determine what should be included in the portfolio. Frieberg and Waxman (1990) warned that ratings of self-assessments tend to be higher than assessments which are made by supervisors. It is therefore important that a database for reflection in self-assessment is established in order to measure teaching. Self-assessment is a reflective practice that becomes more realistic as the teacher gains experience in the classroom. The development of a portfolio enables the student teacher to compare products and provide evidence of professional competency through a variety of mediums.

The last practice/technique that was examined in this study was problematizing. Schön described problematizing as the act of naming and framing a problem. The student identifies what is to be attended to, and where to locate the center for reflection. Adler (1990) suggested that in this way problems that were out of the routine could be identified and then new or creative solutions could be posed and considered.

Addressing the infusion of reflective practices into teacher education is a natural result of the preceding discussion of reflective practices for inservice teachers, and practices/ techniques that are believed to promote reflective thinking. Adler (1990) noted that although there was still little empirical evidence that any of the above mentioned practices or techniques promote critical or reflective thinking, this should be an ongoing conversation in educational circles. She seemed less than assured that teacher educators are really practicing these things in their programs. Sparks-Langer et al (1990) believed that reflection was necessary to connect the concepts and principles from courses to the reality of the classroom. It is only through reflection that the teacher can make a thoughtful and appropriate decision.

Design & Methodology

After an examination of the current literature on the subject of infusing techniques and methodology into teacher education programs for the development of reflective teachers, the following list of practices was compiled based on the most frequent occurrences of listed practices in the literature.

Autobiographical Works
Where students write detailed histories about themselves, and then tie these works back to how they see themselves as both learners and teachers.

Case studies
Where students read and analyze a series of well documented incidents concerning the solving, by others, of real world educational problems.

Critical Inquiry
Where students are encouraged to methodically question actions, practices, approaches, etc... which are otherwise taken for granted as status quo.

Curriculum Analysis& Modification
Where students apply recognized curriculum analysis strategies in order to assess quality and potential effectiveness. Curricula is then modified as necessary.

Dialoging
Where student teachers participate in scheduled sessions with either their cooperating and/or supervising teachers to discuss problems, strategies, etc.

Ethnography	Where students write "biographies" of the school settings where they do their teaching practica so as to understand why the school is the way it is.
Forums	Where students conduct panel discussions dealing with any issue that relates back to the profession of education.
Journals	Where students write regular, ongoing entries into a log reflecting on the events which occur during their teaching practica.
Portfolios	Where students provide evidence of professional competencies through a variety of mediums (e.g. paper, video, diskette, etc.).
Problematizing	Where students define and analyze specific problems in their teaching setting, and are then required to develop solutions for those problems.

These ten practices or techniques then became the foundation for further study of the literature, the identification of the population, and the development of the survey instrument.

This study was descriptive in its methodology. The review of literature indicated that while much has been written about the "reflective practitioner," and even about the infusion of reflection into teacher education programs, little was available to indicate what the level of acceptance was for the various practices, or to what level these practices were currently being used in educational programs. Furthermore, nothing was found concerning the aforementioned points as they pertained to teacher education programs at Christian colleges and universities. As with most research issues, the question of "what is" must be answered before any investigation can be implemented in seeking to address the question "why."

The population of interest in this study was composed of professors of education who taught at Christian College Coalition (CCC) member colleges and universities in the western United States. The professors must have taught at institutions which offered a four-year degree in elementary or secondary education which would qualify graduates for either elementary or secondary teaching licensure by their respective states. Seventeen such institutions were identified using Peterson's Guides (1992), Choose a Christian College. These schools were located in the following states: Washington, Oregon, California, Arizona, Colorado, and Idaho. Each institution was contacted, and the names of all faculty who were at least three quarters full-time equivalency in their respective teacher education programs were secured to constitute the frame. In total, this made up a list of 88 names. The entire population was surveyed. Given the small size of the population, there was no need to randomly select a sample.

Based on the study's first key question, "What is the perception of teacher educators in Christian institutions concerning various recognized practices and techniques used in producing reflective preservice teachers?" the researchers selected ten of the most often listed practices discovered in the literature review and included them in the questionnaire to be responded to by the survey population.

In an effort to address the second key question of the study, "What is the usage level of various recognized techniques and practices for the infusion of reflection in preservice teachers by teacher educators in Christian institutions?" the researchers included in the questionnaire the same ten practices and techniques addressed above so that the survey population might rate their personal level of usage for each item. The questionnaire concluded with a section addressing a variety of demographic questions.

The content validity of the instrument was checked by six individuals from three universities, two from the west coast, and one from the midwest.

Part one of the instrument required the respondent to indicate his/her position by rating each item on a modified 1 to 9 Likert-type scale. This scale was chosen for two reasons. First, it allowed the respondent the most convenience in answering. Second, the 1 to 9 response allowed for an interval scale with a wide enough range to facilitate an adequate distribution of responses in developing realistic means.

Part two of the instrument required the respondent to indicate his/her current and perceived future use of each of the ten listed practices and techniques by circling one of the four options associated with each of the ten items. The four options were as follows:

1 - Currently using, and will continue to use
2 - Currently using, and plan to discontinue
3 - Currently not using, but plan to use
4 - Currently not using, and plan not to use

Part three of the instrument sought to determine relevant personal background from each respondent so that the data could be examined in terms of other related variables. The researchers used a procedure for data collection based upon that which was suggested by Ary, Cheser-Jacobs, and Razavieh (1990), which included an initial mailing of the survey packet, a postcard follow-up, and then a second follow-up consisting of another survey packet. On the official "cut-off" date for the study, a total of 66 returns, constituting a 75% response rate, had been received by the researchers. Respondents were compared with nonrespondents based upon a comparison of early and late respondents as suggested by Miller and Smith (1983).

The first objective of this study was satisfied by individually analyzing questionnaire items 1 to 10 in terms of all of the respondents, as well as in light of various demographic considerations through the use of tests of multiple mean comparison (t-test and ONE-WAY ANOVA).

The second objective of this study was satisfied by individually analyzing questionnaire items 11 to 20 through frequency tables and histograms. Originally, this data was to have been analyzed in terms of all respondents by using a "Goodness of Fit" X^2. It was also to have been analyzed in light of various demographic considerations through the use of "Tests of Homogeneity" -- both nominal data, and k-sample case X^2s. However, the data were such that all too often there were cells without enough "expecteds." Even when cells were collapsed to their smallest possible levels, too many of the tests were nullified by cells with too few "expecteds."

Findings, Conclusions & Recommendations

Findings

Of the 63 respondents to the survey instrument, 33.3% were from Oregon or western Washington, 28.6% were from the state of California, and 38.1% were from the remaining western states including eastern Washington. Sixty-four percent of the respondents indicated that they had taught at the K-12 grade level for between five and fourteen years, with a mean of 10.89 years. Concerning grade levels, 47.6% taught elementary school, 20.6% taught middle school, 25.4% taught high school, and 6.3% did not specify. Nearly fifty-nine percent of the respondents taught nine years or less in teacher education programs, with an overall mean of 9.10 years. In terms of the highest degree attained, 65.1% possess doctorates, and 34.9% possess master's degrees. Eighty-one percent of the respondents hold valid teaching certificates for the states in which they reside. The respondents reported themselves to be 38.1% male and 55.6% female, with 6.3% failing to specify. (Three of the four unreported gender cases occurred in the Oregon/western Washington geographic region.)

The first objective of this study was to determine the perception that teacher educators in Christian institutions have concerning various recognized practices and techniques used in attempting to produce reflective preservice teachers. The respondents believed strongly that all ten reflective practices/techniques listed on the instrument were of value to the aforementioned ends. Autobiographical works received the lowest value rating with a mean of 5.89 (on a Likert-type scale of 1 to 9) still considered to be of "much" value. Six of the ten listed items ranked as being of "very much" value, with the item "dialoging" receiving a mean of 8.14.

The second objective of this study was to determine the usage level of various recognized techniques and practices for the infusion of reflection in preservice teachers by teacher educators in Christian institutions. In every methodology studied, the category "currently using, and will continue to use" received the highest frequency counts. Again, in every case, the anticipated level of usage increased beyond the current level of usage. As a group, the respondents did not expect to decrease the usage of any one of the ten reflective practices/techniques.

After having met the objectives of the study, the researchers believed that it would be valuable to examine the effects of five respondent characteristics on the findings of the study as said findings related to the aforementioned objectives. Respondent characteristics which were analyzed included: state education agency (SEA) certification status, gender, grade level background, degree attainment, and geographic region. In analyses where more than two levels of the characteristic were examined, the results of the Scheffé post hoc multiple mean comparison test (alpha=.05) were considered. With the exception of a few cases, there were no major statistically significant differences noted between levels of the various demograhic characteristics examined.

Major Findings:

Given the results of the research, the following observations are considered to be the major findings of this study:

1. Respondents indicated that they valued all of the reflective practices/techniques "much" to "very much."

2. Respondents indicated that current usage of any given reflective practice/technique exceeds non-usage of the same for 80% of the reflective methodologies studied.

3. Respondents indicated that future usage of any given reflective practice/technique is anticipated to exceed non-usage of the same for 100% of the reflective methodologies studied.

4. Respondents indicated that usage levels were expected to increase for every one of the reflective methodologies studied.

Discussion of the Findings

1. Respondents indicated that they valued all ten of the reflective practices/techniques "much" to "very much." This may not be surprising considering the volume of literature touting the importance of reflective practice for teachers. There is also a considerable body of literature addressing teacher education programs specifically. Reflective practice is a current topic that is looked on favorably by many in the education community. This response is a little disconcerting, however, considering the lack of research on the efficacy of reflective practice, either in the K-12 classroom or in teacher education programs.

   Some of the highly rated response to perceived value may also be a result of the loose definitions for the reflective practices/techniques. Again, Ross (1990) noted that there may never be clear definitions for these practices, or even for what constitutes reflective practice itself.

2. Respondents indicated that current usage of any given reflective practice/technique exceeds non-usage of the same for 80% of the reflective methodologies studied. Reasons for this result may be similar to those given for the first major finding, although this study may be one of the first to document this finding. The consumers of the American education system are expecting better things in the future from teachers and students. Believing that reflective practice may be the current remedy for whatever it is that is afflicting the system, educators

of future teachers are generally willing to try what is recommended by prestigious writers and researchers.

3. Respondents indicated that future usage of any given reflective practice/technique is anticipated to exceed non-usage of the same for 100% of the reflective methodologies studied. Once again, the rationale for the first two major findings of this study may also apply to this result.

4. Respondents indicated that usage levels were expected to increase for every one of the reflective methodologies studied. Future usage will increase to more than half of the respondents for all ten practices or techniques and to more than three-fourths of the respondents for seven of the ten practices or techniques. This may be a result of programmatic successes at individual institutions, indicating that increased infusion of reflective methodologies is advisable. More research needs to be done, and findings shared, as to which of these practices/techniques, if any, are valuable for preservice teachers.

Conclusions

The target audience of this study consisted of the colleges of the Christian College Coalition that operate teacher education programs. The conclusions that were drawn from the study pertain in the most part to Christian college teacher education programs. These conclusions are:

1. Christian college teacher educators favor reflective practices or techniques for preservice teachers in their programs.

2. Teacher-educators at Christian colleges will increase their usage of reflective practices or techniques in their programs in the future.

3. More Christian college teacher-educators will use reflective methodologies than will not use those methodologies in the future.

4. Males may tend to value reflective methodologies less than do their female counterparts.

5. With the exception of only a few cases, there were no major statistically significant differences noted between levels of the various demograhic characteristics examined.

Recommendations

With the conclusions garnered from this study, the researchers make the following recommendations primarily to Christian college faculty in teacher education programs. Their recommendations are:

1. Education faculty in Christian colleges should encourage reflection on why they value reflection. Faculty encouraging reflective practices for their students should themselves be reflective.

2. Education faculty in Christian colleges should determine what it is about each reflective practice/technique that causes them to value it.

3. A determination should be made as to which methodologies most benefit teachers who have been trained in reflective practice.

4. Given content pressures, Christian college education department faculty need to ascertain how much time should be devoted to infusing reflective methodologies.

5. Faculties should devise a comprehensive strategy for infusing reflective methodologies, rather than practicing haphazard methods.

Summary

There has been no research to this point that has addressed the issues of whether or not teacher educators in general believe in and practice reflective strategies/techniques in their teacher education programs. And specifically, there is no research in the arena of Christian teacher educators. Christian teacher educators must carefully examine this topic in order to determine the value for them of infusing a complex series of ideas that may or may not finally produce reflective practitioners for the classrooms of tomorrow.

The purpose of this study then was to determine exactly which reflective strategies/techniques are valued and used by which Christian teacher educators. The intention was to document baseline data on which further discussion of the topic could be built. This study targeted only regular faculty in education departments of Christian colleges to determine how reflective practice has been integrated into teacher education programs.

As far as the researchers could determine, the literature on reflective practice has come from secular teacher education programs and researchers. There are some inherent differences in basic philosophy between secular and Christian colleges, and one would expect some differences in the rationale for infusion of reflective practice. However, the rationale and form of the practice may more easily be discussed when built upon some type of baseline data such as that put in place by this study.

Reference List

Adler, S.A. (1990, Bebruary). the refelctive practitionaer and the curriculum of teacher education. Paper presented at the Annual Meeting of the Association of Teacher Eductors, Las Vegas, NV. (ERIC Document Reproduction Service No. ED319693

Adler, S.A. (1991). The reflective practioner and curriculum of teacher education. Journal of Education for Teaching. 17(2), 139-150.

Ary, D. Cheser-Jacobs, I, & Razaviech, A. (1990). Introduction to research in education (4th ed.)Z Fort Worth, TX: Holt, Rinehart and Winston, Inc.

Canning, C. (1991March). What teachers say about reflection. Educational Leadership pp. 18-21.

Freiberg H.J. & Waxman, H.C. (1990). Reflection and the acquisition of technical teaching skills. In R.T. Clift, W.R. Houston, and M.C. Pugach (Eds.) Enouraging reflective practice in education: An analysis of issues and programs. (pp. 119-138). New York, NY: Teachers College Press.

Miller, L.E. & Smith, K.L. (193). Handling nonresponsive issues. Journal of Extension, 21(5), 45-50.

Noordhoff, K. & Kleinfeld, J. (1990). shaping the rhetoric of reflection for multicultural settings. In R. T. clift, W.R. Houston, and M.C. Pugach(Eds.) Encouraging reflective practice in education:An analysis of issues and programs(pp. 163-185). New York, NY: Teachers College Press.

Peterson's guides. (1992). Choose a Christian college. Princeton, NJ: Pertonson's Guides, Inc. in conjunction with the Christian College Coalition.

Ross, D.D. (1990). Programmatic structures for the preparatio of reflective teachers. In R. T. clift, W.R. Houston, and M.C. Pugach(Eds.) Encouraging reflective practice in education:An analysis of issues and programs(pp. 97-118). New York, NY: Teachers College Press.

Schön, D.A. (1987). Educating the reflective practitioner toward a new design for teching and learning in the professions. San Francisco, CA: Jossey-Bass Inc., Publishers.

Schön, D.A. (1989). Quotations: A symposium on Schön's concept of reflective practice. Critiques, commentaries, illustrations. Journal of Curriculum and Supervision, 5(1), pp. 6-9

Sparks-Langer, G.M., Simmons, J.M., Pasch, M., Colton, A., & Starko, A. (1990). Reflective pedagogical thinking: How can we promote it and measure it? Journal of Teacher Education, 41(4), 23-32.

Zeichner, K.M. (1987). Perparing reflective teachers: An overview of instructional strategies which have been employed in preservice teacher education. International Journal of Educational Research, 11,(5), 565-575.

Chapter 7

Encouraging Critical Thinking:
Asking and allowing good questions.

Patricia Murphy Long

Education Department
Malone College, Canton, Ohio.

Introduction

Jesus Christ was masterful in His use of questioning. The evidence of the four Gospels is unmistakable. The gospels recorded over 270 questions which Jesus asked. Because He knows all, the purpose behind the questioning was not to discover that which he did not know, but rather to encourage those listening to think critically about what they were hearing and doing. Christ did not feel it was enough to just tell. He wanted those whom he taught to "interact with the material."

There is undoubtedly much to be learned from Christ's example as the master teacher. One of these lessons comes in the are of effective questioning as a means to encourage a deeper understanding and conceptualization of information. The example of Jesus demonstrates His ability to ask questions for "higher order thinking." Long before Bloom's taxonomy became popular, Jesus was asking questions to encourage application, evaluation, analysis, and synthesis of the truths he imparted.

As teacher-educators, we have a responsibility to equip students with strategies for effective instruction. Few would argue the need to improve the ability of teachers in the area of questioning for critical thinking. There appears to be a growing urgency for teachers and their students to master the following skills:

- determining the credibility of a source;

- distinguishing the relevant from the irrelevant,
- distinguishing facts from value judgments,
- identifying and evaluating unstated assumptions,
- identifying bias,
- identifying point of view,
- evaluating evidence to support a claim (Beyer, 1985).

It is of particular concern that there are those who would see critical thinking as antithetical to Christian faith, where the acceptance of absolutes and Truth is emphasized. As a teacher educator, for more than fifteen years at a Christian college, I have become increasingly aware of the utter necessity to assure preservice teachers, many of who are Christians, of the need to think critically concerning information presented to them and to compel their students to do the same. By encouraging such, they must realize critical thinking is called critical not because it is negative or accusatory, but because it judges according to prescribed criteria.

Critical Thinking

Defining Critical Thinking

There are many who have tried to carefully define critical thinking. The definitions which follow are but a few of the ones which can be found in the literature. Some have defined critical thinking very broadly. Dewey (1933), for instance, equates critical thinking with reflective thinking, whereas others closely associate it with problem solving.

More narrowly, critical thinking has been regarded as cognitive activity associated with the evaluation of products of thought. This cognitive activity, more accurately called critical or evaluative thought, would seem to be an essential element of problem solving, decision making and creative production. It involves such mental activities as the recognition of information (including understanding and comprehension), the testing and verification of ideas and information and the judging of thought products (Yinger, 1980). Perhaps the most succinctly stated definition of critical thinking was proposed by Ennis (1962) as "the correct (or reasonable) assessment of statements."

All these definitions appear to have in common the idea that a person's critical thinking involves a willingness, perhaps even a predisposition, and an ability to scrutinize and evaluate thinking, one's own as well as others, to determine truth, accuracy, or worth and to construct logical arguments to justify claims or assertions (Paul 1984).

Evidence for Impaired Thinking

An investigation into teaching practices which encourage critical thinking often leads to the work of Louis Raths. As Raths considered the importance of "teaching for thinking," he emphasized the link between behavior and thinking. Raths theorized "certain behaviors of people reflect an incompleteness or inconsistency of thought. These behaviors reflect experience with thinking that has not been adequately rigorous in terms of higher-order thinking operations" (Raths et al., 1966). Practically Speaking, one might wonder what such behaviors might look like when exhibited by students in the classroom. Selma Wasserman (1987) provided a list of these specifically patterned behaviors, identified by Raths, which might indicate a lack of critical thinking, thinking that may actually be "impaired." They include the following.

1. <u>Very impulsive pupils.</u> They seem to act "without thinking." They make decisions quickly, impulsively; thinking in advance, planning, and considering alternatives are not part of these pupils' behavioral repertoire. Pupils who are impulsive will do or say the first think that comes into their heads. They go into action before they "put their minds in gear."

2. <u>Over dependent pupils.</u> These pupils are so utterly dependent that they cannot complete a task without help at virtually every step. They get "stuck" and continually rely on the teacher to give them a push before they are able to proceed.

3. <u>Pupils who cannot connect means with ends.</u> These students' strategies are incompatible with their goals. They may have clear goals, but they are unable to formulate plans and carry out procedures that will enable them to realize their goals.

4. <u>Pupils who miss the meaning.</u> These students have difficulty comprehending. When a direction has been given, they can't seem to follow it. They may ask other students to explain. We fault them for not paying attention, but their difficulty is much deeper. They are unable to conceptualize big ideas or large issues.

5. <u>Pupils who are dogmatic and closed-minded about their beliefs.</u> These pupils are utterly convinced that they are right, that their views are the only acceptable ones, that they have all the answers. Situations in which thoughtful people entertain doubts are the ones of dead certainty for these pupils.

6. <u>Pupils who are rigid and inflexible.</u> These pupils operate within a very narrow set of rules and are unable to break free. They prefer to behave in terms of clearly defined formulas. Change and innovation frighten them. They are resistant to new ideas, new materials, new ways of doing things, and new situations. They prefer to have things done in the old ways, the known ways, the tried and true ways.

7. <u>Pupils who are under confident about their ideas.</u> These pupils are afraid of expressing their ideas for fear they may be wrong. They almost never volunteer a response in class to any question that involves thought. "What do you think?" will almost always result in silence.

8. <u>Pupils who are anti-intellectual.</u> These pupils condemn the process of thinking as a waste of time and effort. They detest independent work, projects, discussions, and research. They are lesson-learners. They believe the teacher should do the thinking and the pupils should give the right answers, which are to be found in the texts. They don't want to be in doubt about standards of accomplishment, i.e. how the final grade is going to be determined.

Christianity and Critical Thinking

Perhaps as the above-stated behaviors are considered, we are reminded of students in our own classes who have demonstrated such, and in doing so, have given hints of "impaired" thinking skills. As mentioned in the introduction of this paper, these behaviors may be exhibited by students who come from and church experiences where individuals warned of the danger of those who would encourage a careful scrutiny of the truths of Scripture. In fact, the truths were to be accepted by faith, without any thought for why they were considered the truth. I was one such individual, encouraged to merely accept and not question. Not until I found myself at a secular university, doing graduate work and challenged by the opinions of very well educated and unbelieving peers, did I realize the absolute necessity of critically examining the doctrinal truths of Scripture. As I did, my faith once again became very alive to me and I felt with certainty that I could give an account of the reason for the hope that is within me (1 Peter 3:15).

There are many instances of interaction between Jesus and others which demonstrate how the instruction of this Master Teacher encouraged individuals to think critically about their own ideas in relation to what they were hearing. In particular, as Christ's teachings are examined, many examples of his ability to ask questions are found. He used various types of questions as he interacted with others. Sometimes He used factual questions to make a point more clear: Luke 20:23-24—But he detected their trickery and said to them, "Show me a denarius. Whose likeness and inscription does it have?" He used rhetorical questions such as the following: Luke 6:39—And he spoke a parable to them saying "A blind man cannot guide a blind man can he? Will they not both fall into a pit?" And he also used questions for higher-order thinking such as the following analytical question found in Luke 20:41-44— And he said to them, "How is it that they say the Christ is David's son"....David therefore called him "Lord" and how is he his son?"

There are many other examples of Jesus' use of questioning throughout the New Testament. But there is also undoubtedly an emphasis, as shown in his teaching, related to the need to be evaluative in thought, and carefully "discern what the truth is." This then would hopefully result in followers of Christ who are established in their faith not only experientially, but intellectually and factually as well.

Encouraging Critical Thinking in Teacher Education

As we work towards preparing Christian teachers to be effective in the classroom, it would seem there must be a concerted effort to encourage these preservice teachers to think critically about what they are learning and experiencing in their training years. For instance, preservice teachers must become aware of who the "authorities" are in a particular field of study and be aware that not everyone who has the opportunity to be published is a credible source. They also need to be able to distinguish a fact from a value judgment, identify bias, and evaluate objectively rather than accept blindly. As preservice teachers become more comfortable and confident in their ability to think critically, they can in turn inspire their own students to do the same.

Much has been written about ways in which teachers both encourage and discourage students to think critically. First, there are several categories of teacher responses that serve to promote thinking (Wasserman, 1987). One way is for teachers to ask students to reflect on their own ideas. Responses of this kind require students to examine the surface dimensions of an idea, to replay it in their heads, and to assume ownership of it. It is felt these "reflective" responses are the core of teaching for thinking interactions. Another way to encourage critical thinking is to require students to analyze their ideas. Those responses call for deeper examination, entail greater cognitive risk, and therefore produce greater tension. Responses that require analysis should be interspersed with reflective responses and should be used in non-threatening ways. Responses that call for analysis include: asking for examples, asking for a summary, asking about inconsistencies, asking about alternatives, asking about ways to compare data, and asking what data support an idea.

Yet another way teachers can promote thinking is by asking questions that challenge student's ideas. These questions require students to extend their thinking into new and unexplored territory. Here the student is at the greatest risk and, consequently, under greatest tension. Challenging questions should be used thoughtfully and sparingly since overusing them may actually inhibit students' thinking. Responses that challenge thinking include: asking the student to generate hypotheses, asking the student to make judgments and specify criteria for such judgments, asking the student to apply principles to new situations, asking the student to make predictions, and asking the student to formulate ways to test predictions or hypotheses.

It is also believed that some responses which teachers give to students actually terminate pupil thinking. This may happen when a teacher inadvertently brings closure to a student's cognitive processing. Such closure lifts the burden of cognitive processing, and students no longer have to think about the issues. This is likely to occur when the teacher agrees or disagrees with the student; when the teacher doesn't give the student a chance to think but does the thinking by showing or telling the pupil what to do; when the teacher cuts off the student's response. Closure is also likely to occur when the teacher rewards or reinforces a pupil's response either positively or negatively. Closure can also take place when a teacher undermines the student's confidence in her or his own idea; the effect of shaking a student's confidence is that this student becomes afraid to offer new ideas, opinions, and thoughts for fear of being put down (Wasserman 1987)

Some types of questions, though they do not bring automatic closure, tend to limit pupil's thinking. These include questions that require students to retrieve information directly or merely lead the student in the direction of preferred response. Although information retrieval does involve thinking, it is thinking at the lower levels of cognitive functioning, requiring little initiative or originality. Students have merely to recall information, not to process it. In these types of questions, the emphasis is on coming up with the single, correct answer that the teacher seeks. Therefore, the student's thinking is limited to a very narrow repertoire of responses (Wasserman, 1987).

Unfortunately, these types of questions are often preferred by teachers because the answers they elicit are less time consuming and the easiest to evaluate. In addition to the challenge of asking good questions, there is the need to listen to good questions as they come from students. I remember one occasion when I was observing a student teacher as he reviewed a homework assignment with his class. The activity was one which came from the textbook publisher and a key of correct answers was included. As the student teacher reviewed the answers to the homework items, one of the class pupils asked a wonderful question concerning the correctness of the given "right" answer. The question demonstrated insight and depth of understanding. The student teacher was also aware that the pupil did in fact have a valid point. I sat hoping the teacher would acknowledge the insightfulness of the pupil and perhaps allow some discussion concerning the point, but instead, the teacher merely replied, "that may be a good idea but that's not what the textbook says." The pupil who had asked the question slumped down in his chair and did not offer another answer the entire period. I felt very sorry for both of these individuals. One had been denied the opportunity to thoroughly practice and find stimulating the act of using keen evaluative thought to challenge a textbook publisher's "right" answer. and the other had lost the enlivening result which comes from realizing a pupil had learned the material so thoroughly that he was ready and willing to take that learning to a much higher level.

Asking and answering are both part of learning. Students need to do both, whether they are Christian preservice teachers or the students who are fortunate enough to be found in their classes. As those who prepare preservice teachers, we must accept the responsibility for asking and allowing good questions in order to strengthen the confidence of our students in the area of their own critical thinking. Then, as such confidence is developed and as students observe teaching for thinking in the college classroom, these preservice teachers will enter the field with a better understanding of the necessity to discourage thinking that is merely a gullible acceptance of claims and encourage a way of thinking that is disciplined, discriminating, and discerning.

98   Nurturing Reflective Christians To Teach

References

Beyer, B.K. (1985). Critical thinking" What is it? Social Education, 49(4), 22-276

Bible, Holy. NRSV. Grand Rapids, MI. Zondervan Bible Publishers

Dewey, J.(1933). How we think. Lexington MA: Heath

Ennis, R. (1985). A logical basis for teaching measuring thinking skills. Educational Leadership, 42(2), 46.

Paul, R. (1984). Critical thinking: Fundamental to education for a free society. Educational Leadership,42(1) 4-14.

Raths, L.E. (1966). Teaching for thinking: theory and application. Columbus, OH; Merrill.

Wasserman, S. (1987). Teaching for thinking: Louis E. Raths revisited. Phi Delta Kappan. (460-466)

Yinger, R.J. (1980). Can we really teach them to think" In R.E. Young (Ed), New directions for teaching and learning: Fostering critical thinking, No. 3, (pp. 11-31). San Francisco: Jossey Bass.

Chapter 8

Teachers as Articulate Artisans

Doug Blomberg
National Institute for Christian Education
Mt. Evelyn, Victoria, Australia

Introduction

This paper is a contribution to a dialogue. It is in part a reply to the responses to my presentation at Calvin College in 1992 (DeBoer 1993). One criticism was that the teacher as researcher metaphor did not sit well with my multi-dimensional epistemological model (Blomberg 1978, 1980); it was suggested that the teaching as craft metaphor, which I had mentioned but not developed, might be more productive. Another was that the model I outlined might well be suitable for graduate students or in-service programs, but not for pre-service teachers, who lack sufficient experience to benefit from an approach which takes concrete experience of teaching as central. And a major challenge from the floor was that teachers in schools would not have the time or the resources to do even a fraction of what I was suggesting by the teacher-as-researcher paradigm.

We need a models of teaching that reflect a biblical view of knowing and learning, and we need these to guide us in the way we shape our programs of teacher education. I will elaborate the notion of the "articulate artisan" and explore some implications for teacher education. I will argue that, by combining a reflective, teacher-researcher component with the craft conception, we can develop a model that cuts through the polarity of theory and practice that has so often undermined the best intentions of teacher educators, and that not coincidentally comports well with a biblical perspective on knowledge and wisdom.

Teachers as Articulate Artisans

Now I acknowledge that the teacher-as-researcher simile has an alien ring to it. Teachers are much more inclined to employ a craft metaphor to describe their work, and talk of "research" is likely to be understood as reflecting a positivist paradigm. But if "research" can be re construed as intrinsic to the practice of teaching craft, we will be able to build a more robust and serviceable conception of craft.

So I am trading in the researcher label--though not the orientation to which it points--for the designation "articulate", and giving up "craftsman" (or the more awkward "craftsperson") for the gender-neutral "artisan." This will enable me to smuggle in a little bit of artistry as well--an artisan being one skilled in an industrial or applied art.

Teachers who are articulate, then, are those who are self-consciously reflective on the processes involved in solving teaching and curriculum problems. This does not imply an ability to enunciate fully the principles of their practice, nor even that any articulation is wholly or mainly propositional. It may take the form of narrative recon-struction, for example. But, in drawing on an etymologically related meaning, I do intend it to imply a critical awareness of the way in which educational situations are *articulated,* in the sense of the joints and segments that comprise the connectedness of the whole. It is an ability to recognise the junctures at which one has to change one's action, to choose to go this way or that, to turn to the left or to the right, as it were. It is an intelligence that is in the hands as well as the head, a sensitivity to the shape and timing of educational contexts.

Thus, "articulate" implies what Dreyfus (1981), in his analysis of the development of competence or skill in complex human contexts, calls component and salience recognition. This recognition is necessarily embedded in a situation experienced as a whole and it is the basis on which good judgments can be made. In the more expert stages of situational judgment, these components are holistically (rather than analytically) and intuitively (rather than ratiocinatively) derived, and understandings are thus tacit.

Hence, the kind of articulation that is sought from the practitioner is not necessarily analytical and ratiocinative. Such analysis is only one mode of reflective judgment. Analysis makes distinctions, but what is important is the relative "weight" that is given to components (i.e., identifying their salience). We may think of the "segment" as the basic unit of teaching. A segment is any teaching/learning interaction that has a recognizable beginning and ending. It is the problem or task that a teacher addresses, the hypothesis that is being tested at a particular point. Teaching segments nest within one another like Russian dolls, from the two sentence question-answer interchange to the one hour lesson, the program for the week or term, the curriculum for the year and the scope and sequence for the whole school. Each segment is a coherent unit that could be lifted from a sequence and replaced with another. Teachers' decisions concern the meaning of these segments and the judicious timing of the segues between them.

It is wisdom that allows one to weigh the elements of a situation and to make discerning judgments. Wisdom is more than the making of distinctions. It consists in knowing the meaning and the relative value of these distinctions, depending on the nature of the project one has in mind. These meanings and values can oftentimes not be transmitted merely propositionally.

Teaching as Craft

Tom (1984) has given an extended and instructive exploration of teaching as a "moral craft". Van Brummelen (1988), in the desire to bring the broader horizons of normativity into the picture, has espoused the notion of teaching as a religious craft. The idea of craft knowledge certainly seems to fit well with a biblical view of knowledge--Wisdom (the very Son of God) is the craftsman at God's side in creating the world (Pr. 8:30-31). It incorporates the notion of responsible action, of hearing and doing the Word of God, but needs to be further sharpened by the prophetic edge that is also part and parcel of this biblical perspective.

A craft such as pottery requires the use of skills in a way that is sensitive to the material being worked. Guided by a design goal, artisans adapt their intentions as they go, so that the design emerges in process. The work of the artisan is characterised by individuality, so that although it is possible for seemingly identical pots to be thrown time after time, what interests the artisan is the variations and nuances that are possible. To *craft* something is to do it with care and flair. Although the merely technical, skill components can be reproduced by machinery, the artistry cannot be captured in mass production.

The artisan employs *reflexive routines*--virtually habitualised modes of responding to situations that are seen to be similar, but with a suppleness and flexibility that saves them from being mechanical. They may be regarded as "production schemes" which are open to the shock of the new (Sternberg and Caruso 1985).

Teaching may be properly (and not only metaphorically) regarded as sharing in the properties of artisanship because it is characterised by the exercise of formative power. It is centrally a *techno-cultural* undertaking: the teacher is engaged in *shaping* the environment (the technical dimension) so that an invitation to learn is issued and *leading and guiding* students (the cultural dimension) with the intention that they learn. It differs significantly from other crafts because of the nature of the "material" with which it works: it is a subject-subject, not a subject-object relationship that is in view. This must be central to our conception of articulate artisanship.

The Traditional Craft Culture

A major problem in *becoming* an articulate artisan lies in how to capture understandings that are in large part tacit and situated, i.e., having some of their meanings distributed across the specific context in which they emerge. Boomer (1985, 17) actually concludes that the composing and acting of a fine teacher are essentially "unmappable" and "ineffable". If so, what are the implications for teacher education?

But the problem lies not merely in the nature of teaching as a context-dependent activity. It lies also in the nature of the traditional craft culture of teaching. This culture understands its peculiar knowledge as "'know-how' encapsulated in behavioural repertoires which are transmitted as common-sense tips within the professional peer group and fine-tuned in trial-and-error experience of numerous classroom settings" (Elliott 1991, 111). This "know-how"--as a matter of common sense--is treated as not really requiring critical reflection or explicit justification.

"Theory" and "research" are deemed irrelevant by this culture. The threat that they might be to conventional wisdom is thus averted, enabling teachers to protect their own private realms of knowledge and to assert their self-authenticating expertise.

The traditional culture largely supports "a non-reflective, intuitive and highly routinized form of practice which [is] executed in the private world of the classroom in isolation from professional peers" (Elliott 1991, 55). Craft knowledge is regarded as individual, esoteric and intuitive, and the norms of the culture are privacy, territory and hierarchy. Such a culture allows teachers to believe that improving practice is largely a matter of developing technique, rather than of confronting the larger issues about the structure of schooling and curriculum (which constrain teachers in their isolation in the first place), of developing an artistry, and of attaining normative goals.

If teachers are to become articulate artisans, this traditional culture must be confronted. They must collegially take charge of the curriculum and the constraints embodied in it. Many of these might be covert, particularly in a country like the United States, where there is *de jure* little centralised control. This is all the more reason why practice has to be critically evaluated, and even more an imperative for Christian teachers, who should be committed to providing alternatives to the prevailing secularist culture of education, whether or not they work in Christian schools.

One way in which this culture can and must be questioned concerns its apportionment of time. If a prime value is that teachers become reflective practitioners, their work days must be organised to allow them to do this. Teaching should not be measured in terms of quantity-
-hours of time in front of a class--but in terms of quality. This is surely the case with any other profession. There will always be "cost-benefit" trade-offs, of course, but a surgeon's skill is and should be evaluated only minimally in relation to how many operations are performed or how quickly a particular operation is carried out; it is similar for the work of a lawyer, an architect, an engineer or a pastor.

This might be regarded as unattainable idealism, but reforms to existing structures only come about as people grasp a vision or invent a new paradigm, thereby freeing themselves from the fundamental beliefs and values of the culture they want to change. Of course, innovators have to recognise that any attempt to transform a culture will be opposed by its gate-keepers, because the distribution of power within an organisation is at stake.

Our responsibility as teacher educators is to consider the contribution that we can make to the transformation of this culture, to consider the extent to which we regard ourselves as its guardians and that to which we recognise a calling to confront it.

An Epistemology of Craft?

The conservatism of the traditional craft culture is an impediment to the legitimation of craft knowledge as an alternative to the epistemological perspectives of positivism, interpretivism and critical theory. Tom and Valli (1990, 390) ask whether it is indeed possible to conceive of the craft tradition in analytic and self-critical terms. The oft-associated notion of training by apprenticeship is held in low regard by educational theorists, because of its lack of analytical rigour. Must education according to the craft conception be a necessarily conservative, non-rigourous mode which encourages traditionalism or can it be a critically reflective, forward-looking practice?

If we are indeed to prepare articulate artisans, they would need to develop metacognitive capacities. Teachers should be not "merely" practitioners, the tools of a technical rationality, but *reflective* practitioners. This is because of, inter alia, the nature of the "material" with which they work. In teaching, every moment is new, because the "objects" of teaching are free to make decisions. Teachers must be responsive to the moment, "seizing the day", as it were.

And because teachers' craft is interpersonal, it has normative dimensions--a "value burden"--that are absent from the work of those artisans that work with impersonal objects. This therefore requires them not only to choose their actions more carefully but also to be able to justify these to themselves and to others, i.e., to be "articulate".

The knowledge that is embedded in the craft culture must be made accessible to other practitioners. But once again, Tom and Valli (1990, 390) ask whether the codification of situated knowledge is a contradiction in terms. Is not the idea of a knowledge base appropriate only in the case of positivism, which "presumes practice to be derived from knowledge?"

Tom and Valli might better have said "derived from theory", but their alternative reflects a deep-seated prejudice in even their relatively sympathetic treatment of craft knowledge, in that knowledge and theory are so easily equated. The question concerns the accessibility of knowledge, without a presumption as to the form that this will take.

The current concern in England and Australia with competency based education can be seen as an attempt to address this question. Unfortunately, the favored model is indeed positivistic, threatening to impose a logical-linear schema rather than to reflect the actual level of complexity of craft skills, the very thing that we should be seeking in an alternative epistemology of craft. The same dangers may arise in the OBE movement in the United States.

Codification of competencies requires the identification of discrete actions, whereas what is most significant about teaching is the flow and sequencing of actions, the context of particular acts in a certain history or narrative. Codification "freeze frames" actions, when what we really want is an understanding of their continuity. Teaching is organic--its various parts have their meaning in the context of the whole--and it always occurs within a dynamic and organic relationship between teachers and students.

Competence cannot be equated with a collection of discrete competencies. To be competent at something will require specific skills, but competence is holistic rather than atomistic. If you remember learning to drive--or have survived the pleasures of teaching your teenage children--you will recollect the importance of attending to the whole, of getting a flow going between the component skills. The good driver is not one who can perform functions in isolation from each other, but rather one who can blend these into a unity. The most important thing about the automobile is that it moves through space and time in a fluid environment, and it is fluidity that is required of the driver. And the good driver is above all a moral driver, a careful, thoughtful, resourceful employer of basic skills. Good drivers get to where they are going with the minimum of fuss, without harm to passengers, pedestrians and other drivers. The skills of driving submerge in this larger project, while conversely, drivers can possess all these skills and be absolute terrors in the way in which they employ these.

Whatever codifications of teaching craft are possible and desirable, these will have to represent the integral, normed, organic and situated nature of teaching. The current interest in case-based and clinical approaches to professional preparation seek to address this imperative.

When Tom and Valli (1990, 390) ask whether craft knowledge can ever be viewed as a systematic way of knowing, they beg the question. They assume that any systematic way of knowing has characteristic methods of inquiry, rules of evidence, and even, without apparent tautological intent, forms of knowledge. This sounds very much like Hirst's analytically-based discrimination of forms of knowledge, which I have critiqued elsewhere (Blomberg, 1978). But might it not be that, recognising craft knowledge as *sui generis*, our task should be the delineation not of what it shares with other systematic ways of knowing--though some overlap might be evident--but of its unique features?

Wisdom in Israel

Articulate artisans will not be theorists in the main, though they may well draw on and generate theoretical insights. Instead, they will be characterised by embedded wisdom. "Wisdom" can provide us with an alternative to the traditional theory-practice paradigm, and the consequent "theory applied to practice", "theory has nothing to do with practice", or "theory is only a kind of practice" models.

Generalizing over Greek philosophy, experience was regarded as totally inadequate to the task of attaining knowledge, which depends in the end on an intellectual apprehension of universals. This is the central point of Plato's Cave Allegory, which pictured what real education would be like. In varying forms, the one message has come down through the Western intellectual tradition from the Greeks: theoretical understanding is the highest expression of human life and the only route to real knowledge.

The biblical perspective on wisdom calls this tradition into question. "Wisdom", in its Hebrew root, denotes competence and skill within a particular sphere. It is at points synonymous with the idea of craft. It is not restricted to those holding a certain position: the manual worker, the sailor, or one possessed of great cunning in political intrigue (II Sam. 13:3) could be described as "wise"--or, we might say, "crafty"; analogously, the fetus that is unable to make its way through the birth canal is "unwise" (Hos. 13:13). The criteria for what constitutes competence and skilfulness are determined by the context in which the skill is exercised.

The pervasive context is the creational order, in all its diversity. Because of this diversity, wisdom does its weighing up of situations under the lead of different normative modes of experience. As Tom (1984, 79) argues, "moral valuations are not the only possible valuations in a social setting. For instance...a person in a social setting may adopt a legal, an aesthetic, or an economic point of view." Distinctions will thus have different valences, depending on the valuational setting.

The Hebrew perspective, unlike the Greek or modern scientific ontology--let alone post-modernism!--presupposes that the world we experience is creation, ordered, coherent and intrinsically meaningful. Consequently, it accords a different role to human reason and action. For Israel, true knowledge was grasped historically and experientially, not above change but in the very midst of it.

Life is properly grounded when lived in faithful response to the order of creation, of which humans are an integral part. The world speaks truth, and this truth is ultimately that of a meeting with God. All experience is a response to him; every action in history's pageant is religious in character. This order is thus not basically rational (which is not to suggest that it is irrational), but is oriented towards people with love. There can therefore be no dualism between social rules and natural laws. Normative order is an aspect of the one world order.

How different this is from the Greek and Cartesian world pictures! It is most definitely a "pre-modern" picture. Rational responses to theoretical principles will not provide us with our ontic security or the basis for right acting; only the law of God in its rich variety can do this.

Whereas ours is an ocular epistemology--we speak of seeing the truth, spectating (*theoria*), reflecting, insight, mirroring nature--the Hebrews' was oral and aural. It presupposed a two-way communication, between a speaker and a hearer, suggesting a greater sense of immediacy and intimacy of contact between the knower and the known. Something is *said* to people by creation; the world order calls to them, inviting them to be guided in all the decisions of life by its instructions. Though sometimes creation speaks as an accompaniment to God's self-revelation (e.g., Psalms. 19:1; 145:10; 97:6), it is not otherwise silent (cf. Ps. 119:89-92). God speaks with the voice of creation as well as through priests and prophets, as his address to Job makes clear.

Enquiring as to what makes knowledge of creation possible and authoritative, Israel answered that the intellect could never free itself from commitment to God. It is knowledge of God alone that puts people into a right relationship with what they perceive, that enables them "to ask questions more pertinently, to take stock of relationships more effectively and generally to have a better awareness of circumstances..." (Von Rad 1972, 67-8). The basic question of knowledge is thus religious: do you acknowledge the God who made all things, or do you serve another?

Where the positivist tradition would have us approach the world seemingly objectively, standing as detached spectators, Israel knew a call to commitment and trust. The end of knowledge was not merely or primarily intellectual. If life was to be lived in all its fullness, facing both its joys and its sorrows, a whole-bodied trust in the Creator and his creation was essential.

This trust is the only basis for action, because action requires a suspension of questioning; one has to commit oneself to a certain course. For our generic Greek, trust was only justified if one had grasped the "eternal reasons of things"; for Israel, trust was not founded in theory, but supra-rational, a matter of faith. This faith is not of a different kind than the faith of the Greeks, it merely had a different object. If for the Greek it was trust in the sufficiency of reason, for Israel it was trust in the sufficiency of God. Because Israel's trust was in a person rather than in principles, knowledge could not be viewed as static and rigid. The order of creation is dynamic, an active response to every word proceeding from the mouth of God and responsive also to the shaping activity of humankind. Israel met the world not as subject versus object across an unbridgeable divide, but as two partners sustained by the one law of God (Spykman 1992).

Though Israel was confident that the world was knowable, it was also in subjection to a God who would never become susceptible to human predictions. This meant that creation could never be finally grasped by humans: there is a mystery at its heart which should lead to reticence about grand generalisations. In the end, knowledge of creation did not depend on mastery, but on submission. While respecting what can be known, it is well not to consider oneself wise, as there is ultimately, "no wisdom, no understanding, no counsel" that is valid in Yahweh's eyes (Proverbs. 21:30).

Here lies the reason why the Israelites could never have coined a term equivalent to "epistemology". Rather than expecting certainty, they were convinced of the continually ambivalent and puzzling nature of events. Wisdom truly was "in history", so that it was not only in her historical thinking, but in all her thinking that "Israel, with great openness, gave precedence to the contingent event over the *logos* achieved by means of abstract calculation...." Every sentence of the wisdom literature was, "in principle, open to any possible amplification. It always had its truth only in a specific sphere in life and in a specific range of comparable circumstances." It was then up to the pupil "correctly to recognise the time in which the sentence is true or in which it becomes false" (Von Rad 1972, 311).

Wisdom then is a matter of *knowing when*, of "matching" precept to context--which is something other than applying theory to practice. It is something other, because the precepts are particularistic in focus. It is *just* action, that is, action that is in accord with the order of creation in its many and varied expressions. It is not the application of theory, because no comprehensive and self-contained explanation of things is possible in a world that is continually open to God. Truth can never become the *object* of theoretical knowledge, because knowledge is gained only in a relationship of trust. Thus, "it is the highest wisdom to abstain from the attempt to control wisdom in abstract terms.... it is much wiser to let things retain their constantly puzzling nature, and that means to allow them to become themselves active, and, by what they have to say, to set man to rights" (Von Rad 1972, 318). The book of Job reflects a "crisis of wisdom", when this openness to puzzlement had hardened into a rigid interpretation of the world as a virtually closed system of cause and effect. This is why Job's friends are able to provide him with so little comfort. They have a simple doctrine of experience, in which wisdom is fossilised. They have forgotten its time-relatedness, that the passage of time presents "a series of life-opportunities to which each human being responds freely and creatively according to the needs and dictates of the moment" (Clements 1992, 51). Having made fixed general rules out of wisdom, they are incapable of dealing with the seeming contradictions experience presents. Though their words might be essentially "true", they just do not apply to Job's situation (Goldsworthy 1987).

The proverbs are not a series of specific instructions for right living, generalisations that only need to be applied. They do attempt to compress experience in symbolic terms, but often in the form of puzzles. They point to the way in which wisdom is to be acquired, as both gift and task. Creation speaks, and we are to respond, by pursuing understanding in the midst of life, seeking out and testing experience (Goldsworthy 1987). We may attempt to capture this experience in words, thus making it accessible to others, but this does not remove from them the obligation of discerning the appropriate course of action for themselves.

Elliott (1991, 52-53) echoes this perspective on wisdom when he says that action research seeks to improve practice "by developing the practitioner's capacity for discrimination and judgment in particular, complex, human situations". This is practical wisdom, "the capacity to discern the right course of action when confronted with particular, complex and problematic states of affairs." Rather than simplifying cases by theoretical abstraction, it uses theory to illuminate aspects of the case that are significant for practice. Analytic understanding is only an aspect of reflection, subordinate to the development of a holistic appreciation. Wisdom is stored as a reflectively processed repertoire of cases in which theoretical and other kinds of understandings are embedded.

Curriculum in Wisdom Perspective

Our conception of curriculum, generally speaking, is framed within the context of the theory-practice schema. To the extent that we can reconceptualise it within the wisdom tradition, we will open up the possibilities of a new and fruitful approach to teacher education. Curriculum is central to the concrete experience of teaching. It regulates how the teacher and the student will relate to one another in exploring an area of the world. It is a continually developing frame within which people set out intentionally to teach and to learn about the world. If artisans formulate designs to produce artifacts, with the two gradually becoming intertwined, then curriculum is both the design and the artifact of the teacher.

Thus, contra positivism, the curriculum is not primarily documents or materials, which might be said to represent the theory about how we will teach, which we then try to apply. This is the perspective that underlies all attempts to have experts devise teacher-proof curricula, which invariably lead to charges of "infidelity of implementation": Job's comforters again! It is reflected in Tyler's (1949) and subsequent rational-linear models of curriculum design, and is founded in the belief that the order of the world is rational in character.

Nor should curriculum be merely an individually determined set of pedagogical meanings without reference to any normative order, as the interpretivists aver, with everyone doing what is right in his or her own eyes. This leads to curriculum design being construed as merely the process of whatever teachers do when they are designing curriculum. There is no meaning except that which is individually or socially constructed.

Nor can the critical perspective be adopted, because the religious root of this is not in the Kingdom of God--the creation order to which we must respond in faithfulness--but in the sovereignty of the democratic community. If only we could be freed from the constraints that are embodied in authoritarian and oppressive structures, allowing full range to ability to practise and name our own reality, then humanity would be redeemed, critical theorists would have us believe.

I think for most curriculum practitioners, curriculum is just what they do. Teaching craft breaks down the boundaries between curriculum and teaching (and learning). In doing so, teachers necessarily respect the open-ended, responsive and personally intimate character of coming to know. Curriculum is part not only of the pre-active but also the interactive phases of teaching. It is what is going on in the teacher's head and in the teacher's hands, and only some of it will get written down on paper, either before or after. It describes and reflects the teacher's intentions, for teaching is always an intentional activity. It respects that teaching and learning are living, growing, ever changing phenomena.

Curriculum is thus an emergent reality, one that cannot be known a priori, but only in process. Thoughts about what the curriculum will be--even a syllabus or a textbook that seeks to prescribe the curriculum--are orientations to action, but not yet that action itself. Curriculum *emerges* in the merging of an area to be explored with a strategy for conducting this exploration. It helps to have a battle plan before embarking on combat, but the battle will develop with essential unpredictability. The spoils will go to the side that is open to its ever changing and challenging form. There cannot be the same correlation between the plan for teaching and the teaching as there is between a building plan and the building (as activity or product) because human interaction is a much more puzzling encounter.

Curriculum is a *timed* reality, involving centrally a *knowing-when*. As a selection and organisation of teaching/learning activities, it must be concerned with the sequencing or timing of activities. This knowing-when is peculiarly the province of wisdom, a sensitivity to the nuances of the moment and an openness to the puzzles and perplexities that call for discerning judgment. Wisdom calls us to listen to the voices of our subjects--both students and content--and to hear in his creation the voice of God.

We can distinguish teaching from the curriculum, but we cannot separate the two. Teaching is the subjective side and curriculum the objective side of the one act, much like the relation between my speaking and the words that I speak. Doyle (1988) has suggested the concept of *teaching as curriculum enactment* as a way of integrating what have been regarded as the two major classroom tasks: keeping order and moving students through the curriculum.

Curriculum is thus dynamic and *problematic* ("constructed, provisional, tentative, subject to political, cultural and social influences") rather than *given* (Berlak and Berlak 1981, 147). This conception fits the wisdom perspective on how we come to know.

Devising and implementing a curriculum involves centrally the selection of strategies for particular teaching episodes, which I have termed "segments". Teachers' planning focuses on the task or activity in which students are to engage (Shavelson and Stern, 1981). Doyle (1983) concurs that the central construct of classroom knowledge is "task". Comprised of a goal, a set of circumstances under which it is to be achieved (a problem space), and a set of resources that can be used to reach it, tasks are accomplished by interpreting the problem space and organizing resources in ways that account for its features. Tasks organise situations for individuals, shaping the way they think and interact with their environments. It is in accomplishing tasks-- responding purposefully to problems posed--that one learns about the world. Being "articulate", then, is not intended to suggest a role *in addition* to that of teaching. It is a call to teachers to reconceive everything they do as the solving of problems or accomplishing of tasks as they progressively develop curriculum. It is through the reflective practice of teaching that the development of curriculum occurs. Improving teaching "is not so much a matter of getting better at implementing an externally designed curriculum, but of developing one; whether it be self-initiated or initiated by outsiders" (Elliott 1991, 54).

School-Based Teacher Education

Hence, it is in accomplishing the task of curriculum enactment that teachers learn to teach. It is this task that should also be the focus of teacher education, though here, unfortunately, "the hidden curricular messages generally communicate the idea that curriculum decision making is not a central part of the teacher's role..." (Ginsburg and Clift 1990, 457).

It follows that learning to teach will require pre-service teachers to actually serve. "All prospective teachers benefit from being taught effective teaching techniques and methods of structuring the classroom. These are not learned simply by listening and reformulating, however. Rather, as for any craft, they must be practised in a real setting--the classroom" (Van Brummelen 1988, 21-2). Either directly or vicariously- -and probably by a combination of the two--learner-teachers will have to join teacher-learners on the job to a much greater extent than is now prevalent. This will change not only the culture of teacher education but also the culture of schools.

Efforts to change school culture are already in place. Professional development schools in the United States are one example. In England, as of 1994, pre-service secondary teachers will spend at least two thirds of their training in schools. This approach is said to *immerse* student teachers in a whole-school environment so that they can interact with experienced teachers for a sustained period. The school rather than the university becomes the focus of the pedagogical component of teacher education. At Salisbury in South Australia, students are interns from the beginning of their graduate Diploma and have as many days in schools as B.Ed students have in four years, in four different co- operating schools. University staff work with students in schools and with school staff to plan student teacher programs (Australia 1992).

These approaches are reminiscent of the Course B Diploma of Education begun at the University of Melbourne some twenty years ago (Dow 1979). This was a pre-service program for graduates, but the principles embodied in it can be adapted to situations where the norm is to intertwine (though usually not to integrate) education studies with other undergraduate studies. I am mindful of Fernhout's observation (DeBoer 1993) that changing what happens in the traditional teacher education sector will have to go hand in hand with reform of the total college curriculum if it is to be successful, but it will be up to teacher educators to take the initiative in this. His comment in the same place that the case study I presented was suitable for in-service but not for pre-service teacher education is also however somewhat ironic, in that one of the influences on the shape of the graduate program I described was Course B.

The aim of Course B was to integrate theory with practice. There were two strategies for this: first, integrate the theoretical courses themselves in relating them to action and second, give students a major and continuous experience in schools during their professional year.

These strategies required the development of close working relationships with schools, representatives of which were also to have a significant deliberative, advisory and policy-making role in the conduct of the course. A major benefit to schools was that they were able to use student teachers to reduce the size of classes and to work with individual students. School staff were also seconded to the University to work in supervisory roles.

The course designers had some strong convictions about teaching. They regarded becoming a teacher as an intensely personal matter;we could say that the artistry and individuality of the artisan was to be respected. A teacher has to discover an appropriate teaching style, grappling with questions like "Who am I?" and "How do others see me?"

They believed that effective teaching requires not only subject-matter scholarship, but a scholarly approach to education as well: the craft of educating requires the shaping of subject matter for pedagogical purposes. Students therefore needed to be led to reflect on the nature and the teachability of the subjects in which they had specialized. Where they had been used to answering other people's questions, they had now to learn to ask their own questions. What in fact emerged was that many of them, after three or four years of specialization, had "a very shadowy and arid idea of the nature of their subject.... As staff, we could do little about it unless we saw what happened when these students were teaching" (Dow, 1979, 11).

As far as their graduate students of teaching were concerned, they were to have as much experience as possible in thinking and acting autonomously, including playing a major part in constructing their own professional studies. They were to be responsible for their own evaluation, largely through the keeping of professional diaries. Coming from diverse backgrounds, they were also to help to teach each other.

The framework for the course was two whole morning or afternoon Methods seminars on Mondays and Tuesdays. Wednesdays and Thursdays were spent in schools--the same school throughout the year. On Friday mornings, students returned to University for Curriculum Studies, a problem-centered course. In reality, the program was much more flexible, allowing students to sort out their own priorities in respect to school and university commitments. The compartments were not neat and tidy, but each aspect flowed into the others. Curriculum Studies and Methods were tied closely to students' teaching. "As soon as one talks about Curriculum Studies, for example, it leads to what is happening concurrently in Methods, to what different students are looking for because of the particular problems they are experiencing in their schools, and to what each of those schools and its supervisors are like" (Dow 1979, 13).

This is of course the briefest sketch; the intention is only to show what is possible, and there are many echoes of Course B in contemporary reflection on teacher education. Dow's evaluation of the course, drawing extensively on student diaries, provides significant evidence of the program's success. Her conclusion is worth citing:

> "There seems little doubt that the mismatch between teacher training and the school system must be met by more school-based courses which bring the two together and help to invigorate both.... Thus the distinction between pre-service and in-service education tends to be blurred.... The future for rejuvenated teacher education and for a 'self-renewing' educational system would seem to lie in strengthening and extending school-based approaches to pre-service and in-service teacher education (Dow 1979, 246).

School-Based Curriculum Development as Professional Development

If teacher education programs are to change by more effective links with schools, then the culture of schools will have to change to accommodate these linkages. By way of example of what is possible if a school community has the will and the leadership, I would like to describe a curriculum development process that provides the time and the context for teachers to work reflectively together, and that would allow for effective integration of student teachers in a professional team.[1]

Mount Evelyn Christian School is operated by an association of parents committed to providing distinctively Christian education for their children, leading to the adoption of a school based curriculum development strategy.

In 1987, the position of Vice Principal (Curriculum) was created and a two-year Curriculum Documentation Project initiated. All members of staff were to be involved in this process, preferably working communally. The Principal devised an innovative scheme: classes from Year 1 to Year 9 would be grouped in threes, with the pivotal grade (2, 5 and 8) teaching the same curriculum in Creation Studies as the year above it in the first half of the year and the year below it in the second half of the year. This "common curriculum" (in two-year cycles) created a large team of two class teachers and three (or more) specialists. The other grades would each have half a year of "age specific" units, repeated each year; these class teachers joined with one or more specialists to form small teams. A Curriculum Team Leader was appointed within each team.

Documentation did not begin from scratch but meant bringing the teacher's working materials into publicly accessible form. The focus was on curriculum development, but development that assumed that evaluation was integral. The concern was less with supporting statements and specification of objectives than it was with what the teacher and students would actually do, with the processes of teaching and learning, with curriculum as "ideas to be tested in practice" (Rudduck 1984, 232).

This required communal evaluation of what had been and was to be taught: curriculum decision-making for formative purposes. Teams met to plan activities for the next two weeks in the light of their reflection on how well students had progressed in the preceding period, which activities had engaged them and which had not, what particular problems in understanding had become evident, and so on. The document was but an artifact of this process.

Central to the document was the section recording "Teaching and Learning Processes." This designation attempted to capture the emphasis on the process of learning (and teaching) rather than on the content; curriculum is by its very nature a plan for action, not merely or even primarily a description of content. It also underlined the *co-*

responsibility of teachers and learners for classroom transactions and their outcomes. The resulting documents were more in the nature of case studies of units, capturing the curriculum as implemented at a particular time. The Project was as much a teacher development as a curriculum development venture. Teachers were called upon to expose their own teaching--methods and styles as much as content--to their colleagues and to be willing to submit themselves to criticism. Teachers became more directly accountable to one another for what was happening in their classrooms. They developed a "community of discourse" as they discussed not the specific behavior problems that tend to supply the snippets for staffroom conversation, nor the administrative matters that can overwhelm staff meetings, but the much more substantive and significant issues of curriculum design.

It is in this kind of context that the idiosyncratic craft knowledge of individual teachers can be articulated into publicly-testable guidelines for teaching practice. It would be a small matter on the part of schools to incorporate student teachers in this curriculum development process. And what better way to build a case literature of education than by starting with the documentation of teachers' enactment of the curriculum?

Notes:
1. A more comprehensive description of this process is given in Blomberg (1991).

Reference List

Australia, Department of Employment, Education and Training. (1992). Teacher Education. Canberra.

Berlak, A., and Berlak, H. (1981). Dilemmas of schooling: Teaching and social change. New York: Methuen.

Blomberg, D.G. (1978). The development of curriculum with relation to the philosophy of the cosmonomic idea. Unpublished Ph.D. dissertation, University of Sydney.

_____. (1980). Toward a Christian theory of knowledge. In J. Mechielsen (Ed.), No icing on the cake: Christian foundations for education in Australasia. Melbourne: Brookes-Hall Publishing Foundation.

_____. (1991). The teacher as evaluator. Curriculum Perspectives, 11(4), Oct., 32-41.

Boomer, G. (1985). A celebration of teaching. The Australian Teacher,

11, Feb., 13-20.
Clements, R.E. 1992. Wisdom in theology. The Didsbury lectures,
    1989. Carlisle: Paternoster Press/Grand Rapids, MI: Eerdmans.
DeBoer, P. (Ed.) (1993). Educating Christian teachers for responsive
    discipleship. Lanham, MD: University Press of America.
Dow, G. (1979). Learning to teach: Teaching to learn. London:
    Routledge and Kegan Paul.
Doyle, W. (1983). Academic work. Review of Educational Research,
    53, 159-199.
Doyle, W. (1988). Curriculum in teacher education. Paper presented at
    the meeting of the American Educational Research Association,
    New Orleans.
Dreyfus, S.E. (1981). Four models v. human situational understanding:
    inherent limitations on the modelling of business expertise. US
    Air Force Office of Scientific Research, Contract No. F49620-79-
    C-0063
Elliott, J. (1991). Action research for educational change. Milton
    Keynes/Philadelphia: Open University Press.
Ginsburg, M.B., and Clift, R.T. (1990). The hidden curriculum of
    preservice teacher education. In W.R. Houston (Ed.), Handbook of
    Research on Teacher Education, 450-465. New York: Macmillan.
Goldsworthy, G. (1987). Gospel and wisdom: Israel's wisdom literature
    in the Christian life. Exeter, Devon: Paternoster Press/Flemington
    Markets, NSW: Lancer Books.
Rudduck, J. (1984). Curriculum development and teacher research. In
    M. Skilbeck (Ed.), Readings in school-based curriculum
    development, 232-243. London: Harper and Row.
Shavelson, R.J., and Stern, P. (1981). Research on teachers'
    pedagogical thoughts, judgments, decisions and behavior. Review
    of Educational Research, 51, 455-498.
Spykman, G.J. (1992). Reformational theology: A new paradigm for
    doing dogmatics. Grand Rapids, MI: Eerdmans.
Sternberg, R.J., and Caruso, D.R. (1985). Practical modes of knowing.
    In E.W. Eisner (Ed.), Learning and teaching the ways of knowing,
    Eighty-fourth yearbook of the National Society for the Study of
    Education. Chicago: NSSE.
Tom, A.R. (1984). Teaching as a moral craft. New York: Longman.
Tom, A.R., and Valli, L. (1990). Professional knowledge for teachers.
    In W.R. Houston (Ed.), Handbook of Research on Teacher
    Education, 373-392. New York: Macmillan.

Tyler, R.W. (1949). Basic principles of curriculum and instruction. Chicago: Chicago University Press.

Van Brummelen, H.W. (1988). Walking with God in the classroom: Christian approaches to learning and teaching. Burlington, ON: Welch Publishing Company.

Von Rad, G. (1972). Wisdom in Israel. Trans. J.D. Martin. London: SCM Press.

Chapter 9

The What, Why, and How of Reflectivity: Rhetorical Specification, Decoding, and Christ's Love

John Chesky
Montreat-Anderson College

To become effective, prospective teachers need to grasp three increasingly complex layers of reflectivity: the *what* (rhetorical specification), the *why* (the decoding process or cognition), and the *how* (the core value of Christ's love). Rhetorical specification, the first layer—indeed, the surface and simplest layer—equips prospective teachers with handles for deciding upon what they must reflect: self, content, method, audience, purpose, and context.

The decoding process, the more complex second layer, helps prospective teachers to understand why teaching begs for reflectivity: that is, because the values-based decoding process is complex and subjective, prospective teachers realize the difficulty of accurately perceiving the rhetorical situation. Finally, valuing Christ's love, the third and deepest layer, helps prospective teachers to understand how to reflectively decode the rhetorical situation: that is, by dropping the inhibiting defenses and resisting the self-serving offenses of our minds, love causes us to see, hear, and perceive more accurately. Below, I explain each of these layers of reflective teaching.

Reflect Upon What?   Rhetorical Specification

The elements of rhetorical specification provide concrete handles upon which prospective teachers concentrate their reflectivity. Rhetorical specification, the specified elements which determine rhetorical choices (see, e.g., Cooper & Odell, 1978; Freedman & Pringle, 1980; Winterowd, 1975), consists of: content, method, audience, purpose, and context.

a. **Content:** What do I know about today's content? Of this knowledge, what parts do I want and need to teach? What do I need to learn? How do my answers change what I might have taught?

b. **Method:** What is my repertoire of relevant teaching models? With which models am I most comfortable? What model best fits what I am to teach? How does my repertoire of relevant models affect how I might teach this lesson?

c. **Audience:** What do I know about my audience? How do I feel about my students? How do I relate to them, individually and corporately? How sensitive am I to students from populations different from mine? How does my "read" of my audience change the possiblilities of what and how I will teach?

d. **Purpose:** To what end might I teach this content? What are my objectives for this teaching event within the framework of my overall goals?   How does my intended purpose change the possibilities of what and how I will teach?

e. **Context:** What is my socio-cultural upbringing? What special occasions will affect my teaching today? (birthdays, holidays, pep-rallies etc.)? How do my socio-cultural context and immediate occasions change what and how I will teach?

Of course, self-reflection on the rhetorical situation is not enough. Teachers must also learn to reflect upon their individual and corporate audience—their students. With a similar list of questions as above, prospective teachers must learn to decode reflectively their students' (a) knowledge level(s), (b) preferred learning styles and methods, (c) values, personalities, and individual and corporate differences(i.e. audience), (d) purposes, and (e) contexts. Such reflection on self and students helps teachers toward an optimal adjustment of content and method.

The Why of Reflectivity: The Complexity and Subjectivity of Values

If only "reading" the rhetorical situation were simple and objective. If only it were not based in the decoding process, training teachers would be simpler. Based in human perception and information processing, decoding the rhetorical situation is, instead, complex and subjective. An examination of the decoding process demonstrates, therefore, the necessity of reflectivity for effective teaching (and the reason why preparing teachers proves difficult). To understand the decoding process we must understand its defining core concept: *Decoding is initially and thoroughly based in our values* . To explain, I begin by defining *values*.

Definition of Values.

According to *Webster's New World Dictionary.*values are what we "think highly of; esteem; *prize*; (emphasis mine). Indeed, from the 16 dictionary definitions, from the scores of operational definitions in research (for an overview, see, Batson, 1994; Rokeach, 1972, 1973, 1979), and from the connotations gleaned from the popular literature, I use just one of Webster's definitions because it captures the driving force in the decoding process. I find it appealing, too, because "prizing" parallel's Christ's definition of valuing as "treasuring" (Matt. 5: 21; for a fuller exposition, see Chesky, in press). That is, the values I refer to in this paper are those internalized and powerful "prizes" (Webster), "treasures" (Christ), and "controls" (Wolterstorff, 1984; Paul, in II Cor. 5:4) which define—often and primarily unconsciously—everything we are, think, and do. Metaphorically, the values to which I refer can be most quickly and powerfully summarized by Christ's Pearl of Great Price" (Matt. 13:45-46)—that for which we risk and sell all to gain a greater prize. Finally, pragmatically, I clarify the term values by asking the following questions:

(a) Upon what do I continually dwell and about what do I intensely worry?
(b) For what do I take risks?
(c) For what do I consistently expend (or more often *deficit* spend) time, money, and energy?

Long, hard, honest, introspective, and reflective answers to these questions over time would begin to clarify what I mean by core or primary values.

When I speak of values, then, I am not necessarily talking of ethics, morals, beliefs, philosophies, or theologies. I refer to these elsewhere (Chesky, in press) as secondary values. Secondary and tertiary values most often arise out of the *stuff* of our core or primary values. I am instead referring to those things, attitudes, ideas, activities, or people for which we demonstrate a passionate—even non-reasoned, inarticulative, often unconscious—commitment. That is, I am *not* calling values that which we say we value but *that which we prove in practice we value*. In fact, I am referring to those "things" which despite our ethics, morals, beliefs, philosophies, or theologies, we return to again and again—so naturally. Indeed, I am referring to those value-driven mental matrices—those "mothers" or "wombs"— which motivate or predispose us to manufacture and emphasize certain ethics, morals, beliefs, philosophies, or theologies. We create secondary values often to counter or to justify our core primary values. For example, a popular preacher, valuing pornography and prostitution, counters this internal value by continually and vociferously preaching against it. Or, another preacher, valuing wealth and prosperity, justifies his wealth by constructing a theology of wealth and prosperity. Such values, then, consist of initiating needs and desires, primary movers, internal driving forces, matrices, the core of the birth of our being and doing.

What, however, do core values have to do with the decoding process and reflectivity? There are three ways values initiate and permeate the decoding process: (1) they focus our attention; (2) they form a processing matrix or schema and (3) because values are idiosyncractic and complex, they force us to attend and to process idiosyncractically and complexly.

Attending.

According to the research in human cognition and communication theory, we can effectively attend to only one set of stimuli at a time (Wolvin & Coakley, 1988; Underwood, 1989). Thus, because an infinite variety of data, stimuli, and thought bombard us each moment, we need a mechanism for deciding to which set of stimuli we will attend. Our values function as our arbitrating mechanism. Indeed, the research and theory demonstrate that we attend primarily to what we value (Bartlett,1932; McCroskey, 1971). Our values therefore ingeniously cause us to attend to that which we perceive as crucial to us. But the same values also perversely cause us *not* to attend to that which might be as crucial or even more crucial to us. That is, our values are not omniscient and thus can steer our attending in wrong directions. As our values deflect the innumerable stimuli inconsistent with, deplorable to, or simply uninteresting to our inner selves, we fail either to attend to them, or if we attend to them, we fail to attend to them fully. We therefore completely miss or only partially perceive important information. In short, our values can blind and deafen us. In part, then, reflectivity forces prospective teachers to be cognizant of their values-based attention; with this realization and with practice, reflectivity might cause them to attend to that which they might not normally attend and not to attend to that which they might normally attend.

Processing.

The research and related theory in **cognition** (Anderson, 1977; Anderson, Pichert, & Shirey, 1979; Underwood, 1989), in **the sociology of knowledge** (Berger & Luckman, 1966; Cooper & Holzman, 1989; Smith, Carey, & Harste, 1982), and in **communication theory** (Anderson, Reynolds, Shallert, & Geetz, 1977; Anderson, et al., 1985; Bransford & Vye, 1989; Brent, 1992; Crusius, 1991; Langer, 1981, 1982, 1984; Smith, 1982;) also affirm the notion that our valuing predetermines how we process information. Through the straining effects of values-based attention, we build in our minds a network of related concepts and ideas, namely, a values-networked schema (see Anderson, 1977; Anderson, et al., 1977; Bransford & Vye, 1989). This values-networked schema, then, becomes our perceptual processing mechanism for interpreting information and for reconstructing reality (Pearson, Hansen, & Gordon, 1979; Rumelhart & Ortony, 1977; Spiro, 1980).

Our schemata affect what we perceive because (1) language and other stimuli bombard us so quickly and complexly (see Finegan, 1994; Fromkin & Rodman, 1988), and (2) language and other stimuli cannot be totally explicit (see Brozo & Simpson, 1991; Hirsch, 1987). Because language and other stimuli assail us so quickly and complexly, we need the framing structures of predictions or hypotheses to begin to make sense of what might be coming. Also, because language and other stimuli cannot be totally explicit, we need to infer (or construct) the missing data. Note, then, that we do not take stimuli into our minds intact; instead, we process stimuli through our predictions— predictions which range from being generally correct to mostly wrong. These predictions can shape or misshape the stimuli. Moreover, we then process the stimuli through inferring the missing pieces and

recasting fragments into a reconstructed and meaningful whole—
inferences which range from being generally correct to mostly wrong.
These inferences, too, can shape or misshape the original stimuli.
Nonetheless, what the research clearly demonstrates is that (1) our
schemata help us to predict and to infer the meaning of incoming data,
and (2) our predicting and inferring profoundly effect our construction of
the gist of stimuli (Anderson, Reynolds, Shallert, & Geetz, 1977;
Anderson, et al., 1985; Bransford & Vye, 1989; Brent, 1992; Crusius,
1991; Langer, 1981, 1982, 1984; Smith, 1982). Our schema, therefore, predispose us to deciding if, how, how much, and to what qualitative extent we will be able to process, store, and retrieve information
(Anderson, et al., 1977; Pearson, et al., 1979; Spiro, 1980; Smith,
1982).

Formed through our core values, these powerfully networked webs
become, therefore, the percolating matrix through which we process (or
predict and shape; and inference and reshape) all incoming data.
Speaking metaphorically, our schemata become twisting grids or de-
coloring glasses through which we see, hear, and perceive the outside
world. Thus, even when we do attend to information, we twist and
contort that information by processing it through our values-formed
schema. That is, when we do attend to stimuli inconsistent with or
deplorable to our core values, because we process the information
through negative and twisting predictions and construct it through
hostile and contorting inferences, we tend to "read" the information
inaccurately. Even when we attend to information with which our
values are disinterested, we tend not to be able to process the
information well because we often lack any helpful predicting and
inferring schemata.

Thus, blinded once by our lack of attention, we are now doubly
blinded by our values-networked schema and its propensity to twist and
contort information to conform it to our core values. Our information,
then, becomes misinformation—or worse, even disinformation. As
Christ tells us, our light, therefore, becomes darkness—or, at best,
heavily shaded hues of gray (Matt. 6:23). Our sound, therefore,
becomes silence—or, at best, heavily muffled "noisy gongs" (I Cor. 13:
1; see Luke 8: 4-18; see also, Chesky, in press). We perceive objects
and people as true, beautiful, or good if—and to the degree—they
positively effect our core values. Conversely, we perceive objects and
people as false, ugly, and sinful if—and to the degree—they negatively
affect our core values.

Constructed through our core values, these schemata (even when
we do attend to stimuli) open, taint, twist, pervert or close our ability

to perceive. Thus, again in part, reflectivity forces prospective teachers to be cognizant of their values-based processing matrix and their reconstructed reality. With this realization and with practice, an informed reflectivity might cause prospective teachers to (1) reconsider their stereotypical predictions and inferences about student populations and (2) process information in a way they might not normally process it, or not to process information in a way they would normally process it.

Idiosyncracy and Complexity.

Core values—those powerful and percolating matrices we use for deciding to or not to attend to information and for processing or mis-processing information—are idiosyncratic and complex. Core values arise from a number of sources: our bio-chemical and genetic inheritance, our socio-cultural environment (particularly in the early years), our stages of development (cognitive, moral, social, spiritual, and personality), salient experiences, and our choices (see, Slavin, 1994; Sprinthall, N.A. & Sprinthall, R.C., 1990). These sources produce disparate core values in each of us because of three factors:

a. Within and among individuals, *each source produces a profusion of possible values.* For example, the experience of poverty might cause one person to value hoarding and another to value generous giving.

b. Within and among individuals, *each source varies in intensity.* For example, one person experiences a racism which produces rampant unemployment, dilapidated housing, and lynchings, while another person experiences a more subtle racism which produces suspicion, stares, and whispers. The former will (most probably) produce a more intense anti-racist value than the latter.

c. Each individual's *conscious awareness and meta-cognitive control of the exact sources, precise names, and measured intensity of their values ranges on a continuum* from unawareness to awareness and from no control to control.

Thus, this profusion of possibilities multiplies idiosyncracy times idiosyncracy and complexity times complexity. Because we each have disparate interacting sets of sources for our values, because we each experience various levels of intensity in the sources for our values, and because we have varying levels of conscious awareness and meta-cognitive control of the sources, names, and intensities of each of our values, we have disparate core values. Thus, in the exact configuration of our values, we like snowflakes are unique. These core values, then, predispose us to attend or not attend to stimuli and these values therefore create our unique schemata. Our schemata, in turn, determine if and how we see, hear, and perceive the communicative situation— ourselves, our content, our methods, our audience, our purpose, and our context. Since decoding is based in this complex of individually unique values, decoding must also be viewed as an idiosyncratic and complex process—indeed even more idiosyncratic and complex than our values. What others have encoded through their complex of values, we then decode through our complex of values. What other's values strained and re-constructed, our values now further strain and re-construct.

Thus, given that decoding is idiosyncratic and complex; and given a view of decoding as an on-going, never-ending, and imperfect values-based process (see, Brozo & Simpson,1991; Finegan, 1994; Fromkin & Rodman, 1988) reflectivity is, then, the undergirding condition of effective teaching. How can teachers be effective without adjusting content and method for a given audience, purpose, and context? How can teachers make sound adjustments without cognizance of the decoding process, including the impact of each individual's values on attention to and the processing of information? Finally, how can a teacher accurately decode without sound reflection on the entire communicative situation and process?

To be effective, therefore, prospective teachers must learn to reflect upon the communicative situation fully and truly to perceive it accurately. They must learn, however, not just that decoding is based in values, that values profoundly affect attention to and the processing of information, and that, as a result, they need to be reflective because their values-based decoding is an idiosyncratic and complex process. They must also learn about values per se. In addition to learning to decode the communicative situation, then, they must learn to deprogram eflectively the values which blind and deafen them to students' needs, and they must reprogram a way of valuing which enlightens their "read" of students' needs, that is, to the rhetorical situation. Simple cognizance of value's limiting effects on decoding is not enough. Our values so powerfully limit our decoding processes that not even a strong conscious awareness and meta-cognitive control of our values will overcome the effect of values on perception. To be effective, teachers must therefore re-evaluate their values: They must adopt perceiving values.

The How: Valuing Love as the Great Perceiver

The core Christian value of love—as defined (I Cor. 13; Phil. 2:1-12) and mandated (Matt. 22: 37-39) in Scripture—enlightens our seeing, hearing, and perceiving. Because love causes us to perceive the needs of others more truly, love, properly defined and then internalized, functions as a perceptual hermeneutic which helps us to decode our rhetorical situation more accurately. I cite three reasons the value of love helps uso see, hear, and perceive stimuli more accurately.

(a) One reason love heightens perception and causes prospective teachers to decode the rhetorical situation more accurately is that, according to Paul's treatise on love (I Cor. 13), lovers realize that at best they will in their fallen state persistently "see through a glass darkly" (I Cor. 13: 12). Lovers continually realize they do not perceive clearly as the pre-fallen Adam and Eve once did, or as clearly as they will one day (then "face to face," Paul writes in I Cor. 13: 12). Love teaches us that people with various bio-genetic compositions, from various socio-cultural environments, at various levels and types of development, through various experiences, and having made—through all this—various choices, have vastly disparate core values and thus perceive reality differently—indeed, idiosyncratically.

Therefore, love teaches the prospective teacher the need for humble reflectivity. According to Paul, lovers humbly, patiently, and kindly attend to and process information (I Cor. 13: 4). Love teaches us James' edict: "Be quick to hear, slow to speak, slow to wrath" (James 1:19). Love also teaches us Christ's edict: "Judge not that you be not judged" (Matt. 7: 1). Love teaches us to be slow and thoughtful—i.e., reflective—in our attending to and processing of incoming stimuli, particularly information about God and people.

(b) Another reason the core Christian value of love heightens our perceptual abilities is that it demands that we fixate on (that is, to value) our neighbors (i.e., prospective teachers' students) as "Pearls of Great Price." Through valuing the valuable (God and neighbor), and by attending to and processing through love, lovers, with time, build love-attending and love-processing schema. Thus, attending to and processing through love, lovers construct reality through love. Since God is love (I John 4: 7 & 16), since God's image and meaning are love (see Chesky, in press), and since the summation of what God asks us to be and to do is love (Jam. 2: 8; I Jn. 2: 10; Gal. 5:14; Rom. 13: 8-10; Matt. 22: 40; I Cor. 12: 31; I Cor. 13: 8; John 3: 35; see also, Chesky, in press; Schaeffer, 1970), a lover's perception is better, then, because it is in harmony with both the Creator's character and the

128 Nurturing Reflective Christians To Teach

intended design of His creatures. In fact, given Christ's life and teaching, I believe that love is His processing value. Thus, lovers' perception, functioning as the Designer's and as designed, functions better.

(c) The final reason love teaches our prospective teachers to perceive and thus to decode more accurately is that love informs us of "a more excellent way" to perceive (I Cor. 12: 31). Love "does not seek its own" (I Cor. 13: 5). Instead, lovers seek God; dying to self, they value Him and His kingdom as the other collective Pearl of Great Price. Lovers also seek what is best for their neighbors; again, dying to self, they in servant-hood "consider others more important than themselves" (Phil. 2:). Lovers, therefore, do not process information (particularly information about God and people) through self-infested and self-invested values, but through selfless and altruistic values.

Thus, prospective teachers as lovers become more perceptive decoders of the rhetorical situation because they focus not on self but on others (Underwood, 1989). They watch, listen, and take in, not merely dispense. They listen to their students and to information, not merely through their own concerns and knowledge; they find a student's learning style, not just their own favorite method; they ascertain their students' purposes, not merely their own purposes; and they dress their minds in their students' contexts, not merely the clothes of their own contexts. Their perception, then, labels not and judges not—at least not quickly or simplistically. Their perception, instead, laboriously reflects on people of inherent worth and dignity. In good part, then, lovers perceive better because they have dropped both the inhibiting defenses which flee from and the attacking offenses which fight against suffering. That is, lovers do not block (flee from) or attack (fight against) the suffering it takes to perceive accurately. Lovers are patient (long-suffering), empathetic (suffering-in), and compassionate (suffering-with). Because lovers are more willing to be "in-long-suffering-with" both God and neighbor, they are then more likely to do the discomforting, unpleasant, unsettling, and uncertain work of attending to people's needs and of processing information from and about them more respectfully (even reverently). Lovers, then, ought to decode the rhetorical situation more accurately.

Love is crucial, then, not just because we are commanded to love, not just because love is the fulfillment of the Law, not just because it is sin's nemesis, not even because it is needed for better individual and corporate relationships. Love is crucial because we are desperately different from one another. Love is crucial because it is the first principle in accurate decoding of God, self, and others. Love is crucial, finally, because it is the basis for sound reflection. Love reconfigures the structure of our minds so that our minds mimic our pre-fallen perceptual states (Chesky, in press). Love is God's answer to the Fall.

Conclusion

The combination of the three layers of reflectivity—the what, rhetorical specification; the why, the decoding process; and the how, valuing Christ's love—gives students, therefore (a) appropriate and concrete "handles" for deciding upon what they must reflect, (b) the requisite theory for understanding why reflectivity is necessary, and (c) the value of love which teaches them how they can more accurately perceive and therefore re©construct their communicative situation. Love is the great perceiver.

References

Anderson, R. C. (1977). The notion of schemata and the educational enterprise. In R.D. Anderson, R.J. Spiro, & W. E. Montague (Eds.), Schooling and the acquisition of knowledge (pp. 415-431). Hillsdale, NJ: Lawrence Erlbaum.

Anderson, R. C., Hiebert, E. H., Scott, J. A., & Wilkinson, I. A.G. (1985). Becoming a nation of readers: The report of the commission on reading. D.C.: The National Institute of Education.

Anderson, R. C., Pichert, J. W., and Shirey, L. L. (1979).Effects of the reader's schema at different points in time. (Tech. Rep. No. 119) Center for the Study of Reading, Urbana, Ill.: University of Illinois. (ERIC Document Reproduction Service No. Ed 169 525).

Anderson, R. C., Reynolds, P. D., Shallert, D. L., & Geetz, E. T. (1977). Frameworks for comprehending discourse. American Educational Research Journal 14 ,367©381.

Bartlett, F.C. (1932). Remembering. Cambridge: Univ. Press.

Batson, C. (1994). A comparison of value preferences of senior business administration students at Christian colleges and secular colleges in the southern Appalachians . Unpublished doctoral dissertation, Union Institute, Cincinnati, OH.

130   Nurturing Reflective Christians To Teach

Berger, P. L., & Luckman, T. (1966). The Social Construction of Reality: A treatise in the sociology of knowledge. NewYork: Doubleday.

Bible (1975). New American standard version. Chicago: Moody Press.

Bransford, J.D. & Vye, N.J. (1989). A perspective on cognitive research and its implications for instruction. In Resnick,. B. & Klopfer, L. E. (Eds.). Toward the thinking curriculum: Current cognitive research (pp. 173-205). D.C.:

Brent, D. (1992). Reading as rhetorical invention: Knowledge, persuasion, and the teaching of research-based writing. Urbana, Ill.: NCTE.

Brozo, G.B. & Simpson, M.L. (1991). Readers, teachers, and learners: Expanding literacy in secondary schools. New York: Merrill.

Chesky, J. (in press). The Christian college: Being or appearing? In Personal faith to public service: Christian higher education., Anderson, Indiana: Warner Press.

Cooper, M. M. & Holzman, M. (1989). Writing as social action. NH: Boynton/Cook Publishers.

Cooper, C.R. & Odell, L. (1978). Research on composing: Points of departure. Urbana, Ill.: NCTE.

Crusius, T. W. (1991). A Teacher's Introduction to Philosophical Hermeneutics. Urbana, Ill.: NCTE.

Finegan, E. (1994). Language: Its structure and use. (Second Edition). New York: Harcourt Brace College Publishers.

Freedman, A. & Pringle, I. (Eds.) (1980). Reinventing the rhetorical tradition Conway, Arkansas: Canadian Council of Teachers of English.

Fromkin, V. & Rodman, R. (1988). An introduction to language.(Fourth Edition). NY: Harcourt Brace College Publishers

Hirsch, E.D. (1987). Cultural literacy: What every American needs to know. Boston: Houghton Mifflin Company.

Langer, J. (1982). The reading process. In Berger, A. & Robinson, A. Secondary school reading: What research reveals for classroom practice, (pp.39©51). Urbana, Ill.: National Conference on Research in English.

Langer, J. A. (1984). The effects of available informationon responses to school writing tasks. Research in the teaching of English 18, 27-44.

Langer, J. A. and Nicolich, M. (1981). Prior knowledge and its relationship to comprehension. Journal of Reading Behavior 13 , 373-399.

McCroskey, J. (1971). Human information processing and diffusion. In Barker, J. & Kibler, R.J. (Eds). Speech Communication Behaviors (pp. 170©173). Englewood Cliffs,J: Prentice-Hall.

Pearson, P. D. Hansen, J. D., & Gordon, C. (1979). The effects of background knowledge on young children's comprehension of explicit and implicit information. Journal of Reading Behavior 11 , 201-209.

Rokeach, S.P. (1972). Beliefs, attitudes, and values: A theory of organization and change. San Francisco: Jossey-Bassey.

Rokeach, S.P. (1973). The Nature of human values. NY: Free Press.

Rokeach, S.P. (1979). Understanding human values: Individual and Society. NY: Free Press.

Rumelhart, D. E. & Ortony, A. (1977). The representation of knowledge in memory. In R. C. Anderson, R. J. Spiro,and W. E. Montague (Eds.), Schooling and the acquisition of knowledge (pp. 99-136). Hillsdale, NJ: LawrenceErlbaum.

Schaeffer, F. (1970). The mark of a Christian. Downers Grove,Ill.: Inter-Varsity Press.

Slavin, R.E. (1994). Educational psychology: Theory and practice. NY: Allyn and Bacon.

Smith, F. (1982). Writing and the writer. New York: CBS College Publishing.

Smith, L.S., Carey, R.F., & Harste, J.C. (1982). The contexts of reading. In Berger, A. & Robinson, A. Secondary schooleading: What research reveals for classroom practice, (21-37). Urbana, Ill.: National Conference on Research in English.

Spiro, R.J. (1980). Constructive processes in prose comprehension and recall. In R.J. Spiro, B.C. Bruce, and.F. Brewer (Eds.). Theoretical issues in reading comprehension (pp. 245-278). Hillsdale, NJ: Lawrence Erlbaum.

Sprinthall, N.A. & Sprinthall, R.C. (1990). Educational psychology: A developmental approach. NY: McGraw-Hill.Æ

Underwood, M. (1989). Teaching listening. New York: Longman.

Webster's New World Dictionary (Second Edition) (1978), Guralnik,D.B., Editor. NY: The World Publish Company.

Winterowd, W.R. (Ed.)(1975). Contemporary rhetoric: A conceptual background with readings. NY: Harcourt Brace Jovanovich.

Wolterstorff, N. (1984). Reason within the bounds of religion.(Second Edition). Grand Rapids, Michigan: Eerdmans

Wolvin, A. & Coakley, C.G. (1988). Listening. Iowa: W.C. Brown.